UCF Writes

Department of Writing and Rhetoric

A Handbook for Writing at the University of Central Florida

EDITORS

Matthew Bryan   Adele Richardson
Nathan Holic   Nichole Stack
Lissa Mansfield   Jacob Stewart
Kevin Roozen

D1247433

FOUNTAINHEAD
PRESS

Our green initiatives include:

Electronic Products

We deliver products in non-paper form whenever possible. This includes pdf downloadables, flash drives, and CDs.

Electronic Samples

We use Xample, a new electronic sampling system. Instructor samples are sent via a personalized web page that links to pdf downloads.

FSC Certified Printers

All of our printers are certified by the Forest Service Council, which promotes environmentally and socially responsible management of the world's forests. This program allows consumer groups, individual consumers, and businesses to work together hand-in-hand to promote responsible use of the world's forests as a renewable and sustainable resource.

Recycled Paper

Most of our products are printed on a minimum of 30% post-consumer waste recycled paper.

Support of Green Causes

When we do print, we donate a portion of our revenue to green causes. Listed below are a few of the organizations that have received donations from Fountainhead Press. We welcome your feedback and suggestions for contributions, as we are always searching for worthy initiatives.

Rainforest 2 Reef

Environmental Working Group

Cover and Text Design by: Carol A. Hill
Photos provided by staff of University of Central Florida

Books may be purchased for educational purposes. For information, please call or write:
1-800-586-0330
Fountainhead Press
Southlake, TX 76092
Web site: www.fountainheadpress.com
E-mail: customerservice@fountainheadpress.com

ISBN: 978-1-68036-115-5

Printed in the United States of America

Table of Contents

CHAPTER 3

85   Citation

CHAPTER 4

123   Revision

CHAPTER 5

CHAPTER 6

CHAPTER 1

Introduction to Writing at UCF

Edited by Matthew Bryan

Welcome Letter from Director of First-Year Composition

On behalf of the Department of Writing and Rhetoric and the First-Year Composition Program, I want to offer you a warm welcome to the University of Central Florida.

You have been required to purchase this writing handbook for ENC 1101 and ENC 1102, the two composition courses you'll take during your initial year here. However, because writing effectively will be central to all you do here at UCF, you should hold on to this book throughout your college career, and even after. To be a successful student, professional, and citizen, you will need to be able to communicate clearly and appropriately and write persuasively and thoughtfully. This handbook we've assembled will serve as an excellent reference for you as you write your way through the university and, afterwards, into the workplaces and communities you'll inhabit.

During your time here, please take advantage of the many writing-related resources and opportunities that UCF offers. You may visit the **University Writing Center** (in person, or virtually; on the main campus in Orlando or at branches at the Rosen Library, Eastern Florida State College, and Daytona State College) for one-on-one writing consultations, utilize the University Libraries for your research needs, join campus organizations that offer regular opportunities to write, and contribute to student-authored journals like **Stylus**: *A Journal of First-Year Writing* or the **UCF Undergraduate Research Journal**. You may also take upper-level writing courses such as Professional Writing, Rhetoric and Civic Engagement, and Writing for Digital Environments that are part of a B.A. or minor in Writing and Rhetoric, or the Certificate in Public and Professional Writing. Please also feel free to contact us at the Department of Writing and Rhetoric if you're interested in creating additional resources and opportunities for students on campus and those who live in the communities surrounding UCF.

We want to encourage you to consider submitting one of your ENC 1101 or 1102 papers to *Stylus*, our peer-reviewed journal for first-year writers, or to the **Knights Write Showcase**, our annual celebration of student writing. The best papers published in *Stylus* each year are eligible for monetary prizes, and publication is an excellent way to demonstrate experience and credibility on your résumé.

I hope you enjoy your time at UCF, and I encourage you to make a conscious effort to grow as a writer while you are here.

Kevin Roozen, PhD
Associate Professor
Director of First-Year Composition, Department of Writing and Rhetoric

What Is First-Year Composition at UCF?

First-Year Composition Course Descriptions

Composition I and II will likely be two of the first courses you will take at UCF, and you might be wondering what they are about. You might be thinking that you have already taken all of the English or writing classes you could ever need, so what else is there to learn? The course descriptions below were created by teachers in the First-Year Composition Program to explain the ideas at the center of these classes as well as what students do in them. As you read, think about what you've done and learned in previous writing classes and how Composition I and II seem similar to or different from those earlier experiences.

ENC 1101: Composition I Course Description

ENC 1101 develops students' knowledge of what writing is and how it functions in the world. By examining writing as an object of study, the ENC 1101 curriculum invites students to understand their writing as situated within academic, professional, civic, and personal contexts and to develop their identities and abilities as writers across these settings. The reading and writing tasks featured in ENC 1101—such as analyses of writing processes and practices, patterns of *literacy sponsorship*, and conceptions of writing—provide the frameworks students will use to explore the writing they do throughout their lives, how it is accomplished, and the various roles and functions it serves. In addition to helping students interrogate and expand their understanding of writing and writers, these frameworks will allow students to continually adapt their writing-related knowledge and abilities to the new writing situations they'll encounter throughout college and beyond.

ENC 1101 immerses students in the work of:

- Understanding writing as a continual process of making meaning.
- Applying concepts from writing studies to recognize the richly *literate* lives they lead and the wealth of writing-related knowledge they already possess.
- Deepening and expanding their ideas about writing and the work it does in the world.
- Navigating the complex texts emerging from the scholarship on writing, *rhetoric,* and language.
- Analyzing their identities as writers and the processes, practices, and technologies they use for writing in their academic, professional, civic, and personal lives.
- Participating in writing as a social activity through reading, collaboration, peer review, and other forms of feedback.
- Assembling a *portfolio* that showcases both writing processes and products from a variety of genres and that demonstrates writing development throughout the semester.

ENC 1102: Composition II Course Description

Building on the key concepts of writing and rhetoric emphasized in ENC 1101, ENC 1102 further strengthens students' understanding of the work that writing and *research* do in the world. The primary and secondary research at the heart of ENC 1102's semester-long inquiry projects invites students to identify, analyze, and contribute effectively to the complex, real-world *rhetorical situations* that animate their academic, professional, civic, and personal lives. Through a sequence of writing and research tasks, students learn to continually revisit earlier ideas, refine emergent findings and questions, and trace the development of ideas and arguments across multiple sources and *genres*. In addition to generating new knowledge, the research process also occasions opportunities for students to interrogate and revise their own conceptions of writing and research.

ENC 1102 immerses students in the work of:

- Using concepts from writing and rhetoric to identify and analyze complex, real-world rhetorical situations that animate academic, professional, civic, and personal life.
- Considering the technologies and *research methods* (both primary and secondary) that mediate writing, research, and the construction of knowledge.
- Conducting appropriate *primary* and *secondary* research to understand the rhetorical situations that are the focus of inquiry and to situate that inquiry in scholarly conversations.
- Evaluating, analyzing, and responding to arguments that constitute complex real-world *exigencies*.
- Engaging with writing as a process that develops over time through peer and teacher feedback and multiple revisions.
- Employing revising and editing practices to produce texts that intervene effectively in a variety of rhetorical situations.
- Assembling a portfolio that showcases both writing processes and products from a variety of genres and that demonstrates writing development throughout the semester.

What These Course Descriptions Mean for You

One aspect of these descriptions you might notice right away is their emphasis on the study of writing generally and your writing, in particular. As such, Composition I and II are not simply classes in which you will write. You will do plenty of that, but you will also learn *about* writing. You might be surprised to learn that there is a whole field of researchers dedicated to the study of writing, just like there are chemists who study chemistry or astronomers who study the stars. Writing researchers take up questions about writing and how writing works that may be similar to questions you have asked yourselves over the years: Where do writers get their ideas? How do different writers compose? How do writers know their work is "good"? Why do the expectations for writing seem to change so much from situation to situation, sometimes frustratingly so? These are just some of the questions that the researchers in the field of ***writing studies*** attempt to answer.

The composition courses you will be taking at UCF build out of this research, and you and your classmates will investigate similar questions. While we cannot predict now with complete accuracy what the writing you will need to do in the future will look like—a family physician obviously writes different sorts of texts than an aerospace engineer, but they both write frequently—it is a pretty safe bet that, no matter what you end up doing, you're going to write and that writing will figure in your success. It probably won't look like a five-paragraph essay, but the specific expectations and conventions will vary situation to situation. This is why Composition I and II focus on learning about writing rather than teaching you exactly how to write. That way, by the end of each class, you will have acquired some useful skills and ideas about how writing works that should help you when you enter those writing situations that matter to you.

These course descriptions are your teachers' attempts to explain both what they value in a writing class and what Composition I and II, in particular, are about. In addition to these descriptions, we felt it was important to include here some student perspectives as well. After all, these courses are very much about *you*, the student, and what you can learn about writing in order to help you succeed in the situations that matter to you. As you read the student comments on the next page, consider how they seem to emphasize or restate some of the ideas in the course descriptions. Also, what qualities of the classes sound interesting or useful to you? What do these comments lead you to want to learn more about?

What Do Students Say?

"The First-Year Composition Program at UCF has empowered me as both a writer and a person, enabling me not only to find my voice but to know how to express it in writing. Being capable of employing critical self-examination, unpacking horrifyingly dense academic texts, and constructively utilizing feedback and audience awareness is invaluable in academic writing in any discipline and beyond."

Gabrielle Casey, Interdisciplinary Studies, Class of 2016

"These classes not only prepare you to conduct your own research, but they also prepare you for what a college course is really like. They say writing a research paper is like running a marathon. It's a long road, but once it's completed you'll feel like a champion crossing the finish line."

Christina Coffee, Radio-Television, Class of 2016

"At UCF, your composition should be messy. Writing mistakes are good—they're learning opportunities that'll hopefully transform your conceptions of composition."

Mikael R., Writing and Rhetoric, Class of 2015

"Reading and obtaining information from scholarly articles became much easier for me. I have read academic writing in other classes since then and it was not intimidating or confusing at all."

Jacob Vogelbacher, Digital Media, Class of 2017

"The first-year composition classes at UCF are some of the most excellent programs I have ever been involved in. The pedagogical benefits of allowing students to incorporate their own disciplinary interests into the field of rhetoric and composition has insurmountable value that is sure to help students in whichever field they choose to pursue. Students gain a proficiency in building upon areas of their own disciplinary fields that provides both academic and social relevance."

Daniel Huang, Biomedical Sciences, Class of 2017

"The writing program is really a journey into the art and science of communication. I thought I knew what to expect, but I was utterly and pleasantly surprised. This isn't your mother's comp program.... This is 'take it to the real world' stuff."

Komysha Hassan, Political Science Pre-Law, Class of 2017

At this point, you might be wondering what it looks like to investigate writing and why researchers choose to do so. We think that studying writing and *literacy* (reading and writing in all their forms, and the skills needed to do so) produces new knowledge that can be useful for thinking about our own experiences as readers and writers. We can learn a lot about writing by paying close attention to how individuals write, why they write, and the sorts of concerns they are thinking about while writing. At the same time, attending closely to the situations in which individuals write—including the social and cultural contexts that shape writing and the activities in which writing is used—can lead to useful insights about how writing actually does work in the world. You can read about some methods to investigate writing in **Chapter 2**. To give you some idea of what this research can look like, we have provided below an example of an article written by a professional writing researcher.

· ·

"Becoming Literate: A Lesson from the Amish"
by Andrea R. Fishman

Fishman, Andrea R. "Becoming Literate: A Lesson from the Amish." *The Right to Literacy*. Ed. Andrea A. Lunsford, Helene Moglen, and James Slevin. New York: Modern Language Association, 1990. 29-38. Print. Reprinted with permission.

Andrea R. Fishman was an English teacher at Carlisle Senior High School in Carlisle, Pennsylvania when she first published this article. In it, she uses careful observation to document and analyze some of the moments of literacy instruction in the life of Eli Fisher, Jr., a six-year-old boy being raised in an Old Order Amish community. Importantly, Fishman does not limit her study to only what Eli was learning in school. Instead, she considers, too, the wealth of encounters with reading and writing Eli has at home and as part of a larger Amish community. In doing so, Fishman is able to paint a picture of what reading and writing (and learning about reading and writing) mean in one specific community as well as call attention to the literacy-related ideas and experiences students from all social groups (what Fishman calls "mainstream society") bring with them to school. Fishman eventually argues that teachers "need to realize that students, even first-graders, have been reading the world—if not the word—for at least five, six, or seven years; they come to school not devoid of knowledge and values but with a clear sense of what their world demands and requires, including what, whether, and how to read and write, though their understandings may differ significantly from our own"(**15**).

This claim—and the evidence Fishman compiles along the way to support it—has significant implications for the work you will be doing in your composition classes at UCF. For one, the notion that reading and writing *can* be defined and understood differently depending on the context is central to learning how to adapt your writing to new situations. Second, Eli's experiences remind us that individuals (including you) learn about reading and writing from places other than school, and those sources of information can serve as valuable assets that can be drawn on when learning to write for new communities and contexts. Finally, Fishman's article demonstrates one way that researchers can investigate writing to learn more about how it does work in the world. We hope, then, that this piece will give you some helpful inspiration as you begin your own research into writing.

1   One clear, frost-edged January Sunday night, two families gathered for supper and an evening's entertainment. One family—mine—consisted of a lawyer, a teacher, and their twelve-year-old son; the other family—the Fishers—consisted of Eli and Anna, a dairy farmer and his wife, and their five children, ranging in age from six to seventeen. After supper in the Fisher's large farm kitchen—warmed by a wood stove and redolent of the fragrances of chicken corn soup, homemade bread, and freshly baked apples—the table was cleared and an additional smaller one set up to accommodate games of Scrabble, double Dutch solitaire, and dominoes. As most of us began to play, adults and children randomly mixed, Eli Fisher, Sr., settled into his brown leather recliner with the newspaper, while six-year-old Eli, Jr., plopped on the corner of the couch nearest his father with a book.

2   Fifteen or twenty minutes later, I heard Eli, Sr., ask his son, "Where are your new books?" referring to a set of outgrown Walt Disney books we had brought for little Eli and his seven-year-old brother, Amos. Eli, Jr., pointed to a stack of brightly colored volumes on the floor, from which his father chose *Lambert, the Sheepish Lion*. As Eli, Jr., climbed onto the arm of the recliner and snuggled against his father, Eli, Sr., began reading the book out loud in a voice so commandingly dramatic that soon everyone was listening to the story, instead of playing their separate games. Broadly portraying the roles of both Lambert and his lioness mother and laughing heartily at the antics of the cub who preferred cavorting with the sheep to stalking with the lions, Eli held his enlarged audience throughout the rest of the story.

3   As most of us returned to our games when he finished reading, Eli, Sr., asked of anyone and everyone, "Where's the *Dairy*?" Daniel, the Fishers' teenage son, left his game and walked towards his father. "It's in here," he said, rummaging through the newspapers and magazines in the rack beside the couch until he found a thick newsletter called *Dairy World*, published by the Independent Buyers Association, to which Eli belonged.

4   Eli leafed through the publication, standing and walking toward the wood stove as he did. Leaning against the wall, he began reading aloud without preface. All conversation stopped as everyone once again attended to Eli's loudly expressive reading voice, which said:

    A farmer was driving his wagon down the road. On the back was a sign which read: "Experimental Vehicle. Runs on oats and hay. Do not step in exhaust."

5   Everyone laughed, including Eli, Sr., who then read the remaining jokes on the humor page to his attentive audience. All our games forgotten, we shared the best and the worst riddles and jokes we could remember until it was time for bed.

6   Occasions like this one occur in many homes and have recently attracted the interest of family literacy researchers (Heath; Taylor; Wells). The scene at the Fishers could have been the scene in any home where parents value reading and

writing and want their children to value them as well. It would not be surprising if Eli and Anna, like other literacy-oriented parents, read bedtime stories to their children, helped with their homework, and encouraged them to attain high school diplomas, if not college degrees. But Eli and Anna do none of these things: they read no bedtime stories, they are annoyed if their children bring schoolwork home, and they expect their children to go only as far in school as they did themselves, as far as the eighth grade.

7   So, although Eli and Anna appeared on that Sunday night to be ideal pro-literacy parents, they may not be, according to commonly described standards, and one significant factor may account for their variations from the supposed ideal: Eli and Anna are not mainstream Americans but are Old Order Amish, raising their family according to Old Order tradition and belief. The Sunday night gathering I just described took place by the light of gas lamps in a house without radio, stereo, television, or any other electrical contrivance. Bedtime in that house is more often marked by singing or silence than by reading. Schoolwork rarely enters there because household, field, and barn chores matter more. And the Fisher children's studying is done in a one-room, eight-grade, Old Order school taught by an Old Order woman who attended the same kind of school herself. So while Eli, Jr., like his siblings, is learning the necessity and the value of literacy, what literacy means to him and the ways in which he learns it may differ in both obvious and subtle ways from what it means and how it's transmitted to many mainstream children, just as Eli's world differs from theirs, both obviously and subtly.

8   As suggested earlier, Eli, Jr., lives in a house replete with print, from the kitchen bulletin board to the built-in bookcases in the playroom to the tables and magazine rack in the living room. There are children's classics and children's magazines. There are local newspapers, shoppers' guides, and other adult periodicals. And there are books of children's Bible stories, copies of the King James Version of the Bible, and other inspirational volumes, none of which mark the Fishers' home as notably different from that of many other Christian Americans.

9   Yet there are differences, easily overlooked by a casual observer but central to the life of the family and to their definition of literacy. One almost invisible difference is the sources of these materials. Eli and Anna attempt to carefully control the reading material that enters their home. Anna buys books primarily from a local Christian bookstore and from an Amish-operated dry good store, both of which she trusts not to stock objectionable material. When she sees potentially interesting books in other places—in the drugstore, in the book and card shop, or at a yard sale—she uses the publishers' name as a guide to acceptable content. Relatives and friends close to the family also supply appropriate titles both as gifts and as recommendations, which Anna trusts and often chooses to follow up.

10   Another, slightly more visible difference comes in the form of books and periodicals around the Fisher house that would not be found in many mainstream, farm, or Christian homes. Along with the local newspaper in the rack beside the couch are issues of *Die Botschaft*, which describes itself as "A Weekly Newspaper Serving Old Order Amish Communities Everywhere." On the desk is a copy of *The Amish Directory* , which alphabetically lists all the Amish living in Pennsylvania and

Maryland by nuclear family groups, giving crucial address and other information, along with maps of the eighty-seven church districts included.

11   On top of the breakfront in the sitting area are copies of song books, all in German: some for children, some for adults, and one—the *Ausbund*—for everyone, for this is the church hymnal, a collection of hymns written by tortured and imprisoned sixteenth-century Anabaptists about their experiences and their faith. Kept with these songbooks is a German edition of the Bible and a copy of the *Martyrs Mirror*, an oversized, weighty tome full of graphic descriptions in English of the tortured deaths of early Anabaptists, each illustrated by a black-and-white woodcut print.

12   Despite what may seem to be the esoteric nature of these texts, none remain in their special places gathering dust, for all are used regularly, each reinforcing in a characteristic way the Amish definition of literacy and each facilitating the image Eli, Jr., has of himself as literate.

13   Because singing is central to Amish religious observance and expression, the songbooks are used frequently by all members of the family. Because singing requires knowing what is in the text and because Amish singing, which is unaccompanied and highly stylized, requires knowing how to interpret the text exactly as everyone else does, the songbooks represent a kind of reading particularly important to the community, a kind that must be mastered to be considered literate. Yet because singing may mean holding the text and following the words as they appear or it may mean holding the text and following the words from memory or from others' rendition, children of Eli's age and younger all participate, appearing and feeling as literate as anyone else.

14   Functioning similarly are the German Bible and the *Martyrs Mirror*. Though only the older Fishers read that Bible, they do so regularly and then share what they've read with their children. It is the older Fishers, too, who read the *Martyrs Mirror*, but that text Eli, Sr., usually reads aloud during family devotions, so that Anna and all the children, regardless of age, participate similarly through his oral presentations.

15   While it may seem easier to accept such variant definitions of reading in shared communal situations like these, the participation of Eli, Jr., was equally welcome and equally effective in shared individual reading. When individual oral reading was clearly text-bound, as it is during family devotions, Eli was always enabled to participate in ways similar to his brothers' and sisters', making him a reader like them. When all the Fishers took turns reading the Bible aloud, for example, someone would read Eli's verse aloud slowly, pausing every few words, so that he could repeat what was said and thereby take his turn in the rotation.

16   When the older children were assigned Bible verses or *Ausbund* hymn stanzas to memorize, Eli was assigned the same one as Amos, the sibling closest in age. Their assignment would be shorter and contain less complex vocabulary than the one the older children got, yet Amos and Eli would also practice their verse together, as the older children did, and would take their turns reciting, as the older children did, making Eli again able to participate along with everyone else.

17   Because oral reading as modeled by Eli, Sr., is often imitated by the others, Eli, Jr., always shared his books by telling what he saw or knew about them. No one

ever told him that telling isn't the same as reading, even though they may look alike, so Eli always seemed like a reader to others and felt like a reader himself. When everyone else sat reading or playing or playing reading-involved games in the living room after supper or on Sunday afternoons, Eli did the same, to no one's surprise, to everyone's delight, and with universal, though often tacit, welcome and approval. When the other children received books as birthday and Christmas presents, Eli received them too. And when he realized at age six that both of his brothers had magazine subscriptions of their own, Eli asked for and got one as well. Eli never saw his own reading as anything other than real; he did not see it as make-believe or bogus, and neither did anyone else. So, despite the fact that before he went to school Eli, Jr., could not read according to some definitions, he always could according to his family's and his own.

18   Just as all the Fishers read, so they all write, and just as Eli was enabled to define reading in a way that made him an Amish reader, so he could define writing in a way that made him an Amish writer. Letter writing has always been a primary family activity and one central to the Amish community. Anna writes weekly to *Die Botschaft*, acting as the scribe from her district. She, Eli, Sr., and sixteen-year-old Sarah all participate in circle letters, and the next three children all write with some regularity to cousins in other Amish settlements.

19   Yet, no matter who is writing to whom, their letters follow the same consistently modeled Amish format, beginning with "Greetings...," moving to recent weather conditions, then to family and community news of note, and ending with a good-bye and often a philosophical or religious thought. I've never seen anyone in the community instructed to write this way, but in the Fisher family, letters received and even letters written are often read out loud, and though this oral sharing is done for informative rather than instructive purposes, it provides an implicit model for everyone to follow.

20   With all the other family members writing letters, reading them out loud, and orally sharing those they have received, Eli, Jr., wanted to write and receive letters, too, and no one said he couldn't. When he was very young, he dictated his messages to Sarah and drew pictures to accompany what she wrote down for him. Then, even before he started school, Eli began copying the dictated messages Sarah recorded, so that the letters would be in his own hand, as the drawings were.

21   Other forms of writing also occur in the Fisher household for everyone to see and use. Greeting cards, grocery lists, bulletin board reminders, and bedtime notes from children to absent parents were all part of Eli's life to some extent, and his preschool writing and drawing always adorned the refrigerator, along with the school papers of his brothers and sisters.

22   In addition, the Fishers played writing-involved games—including Scrabble and Boggle—in which everyone participated, as the family revised the rules to suit their cooperative social model and their definition of literacy. In any game at the Fishers, the oldest person or persons playing may assist the younger ones. No question of fairness arises unless only some players go unaided. Older players, too, may receive help from other players or from onlookers. Score is always kept, and, while some moves are ruled illegal, age or aid received neither bars nor assures a winner. Eli, Jr., therefore, has always played these games as well as anyone else.

23   Obviously, Eli, Jr., learned a great deal about literacy from all these preschool experiences, but what he learned went far beyond academic readiness lessons. More important, Eli learned that literacy is a force in the world—his world—and it is a force that imparts power to all who wield it. He could see for himself that reading and writing enable people as old as his parents and as young as his siblings to fully participate in the world in which they live. In fact, it might have seemed to him that, to be an Amish man, one must read and write, and to be a Fisher, one must read and write as well.

24   So, even before the age of six, Eli began to recognize and acquire the power of literacy, using it to affiliate himself with the larger Amish world and to identify himself as Amish, a Fisher, a boy, and Eli Fisher, Jr. However, what enabled Eli to recognize all these ways of defining and asserting himself through literacy was neither direct instruction nor insistence from someone else. Rather, it was the ability that all children have long before they can read and write print text, the ability, as Friere puts it, "to read the world." "It is possible," Friere asserts, "to view objects and experiences as texts, words, and letters, and to see the growing awareness of the world as a kind of reading, through which the self learns and changes" (6). Eli, Jr., clearly illustrates this understanding of how children perceive and comprehend the seemingly invisible text of their lives. What he came to understand and accept this way were the definition and the role of print literacy as his society and culture both consciously and tacitly transmit them.

25   When Eli, Jr., began school, therefore, he was both academically and socially ready to begin. To smooth the transition from home to school, Eli's teacher—like most in Old Order schools—held a "preschool day" in the spring preceding his entry to first grade. On that day, Eli and Mary, the two prospective first-graders in Meadow Brook School, came to be initiated as "scholars." Verna, their teacher, had moved the two current first-graders to other seats, clearing the two desks immediately in front of hers for the newcomers; all that day Mary and Eli sat in the first-grade seats, had "classes," and did seatwork like all the other children. They seemed to know they were expected to follow the rules, to do what they saw others doing, to practice being "scholars," and Verna reinforced that notion, treating those two almost as she would anyone else.

26   To begin one lesson, for example, "Let's talk about bunnies," she instructed, nodding her head toward the two littlest children, indicating that they should stand beside her desk. She then showed them pictures of rabbits, with the word *bunnies* and the number depicted indicated in word and numeral on each picture. After going through the pictures, saying, "three bunnies," "four bunnies," and having the children repeat after her, Verna asked three questions and got three choral answers.

"Do bunnies like carrots?" she asked.

"Yes," the *two* children answered together.

"Do they like lettuce?"

"Yes."

"Do they sometimes get in Mother's garden?"

"Yes."

27 Were it not for some enthusiastic head nodding, Eli, Jr., and Mary could have been fully matriculated students.

28 When she was ready to assign seatwork, Verna gave the preschoolers pictures of bunnies to color and asked, "What do we do first? Color or write our names?"

29 "Write our names," the pair chorused, having practiced that skill earlier in the day.

30 "Yes, we always write our names first. Go back to your desk, write your name, then color the picture. Do nothing on the back of the paper." And the children did exactly that, doing "what we do" precisely "the way we do it."

31 Verna also conducted what she called a reading class for the two preschoolers, during which they sat, and she held an open picture book facing them. Talking about the pictures, Verna made simple statements identifying different aspects of and actions in the illustrations. After each statement Verna paused, and the children repeated exactly what she had said. The oral text accompanying one picture said:

> Sally is eating chips and watching TV.
>
> Sally has a red fish.
>
> Sally has spilled the chips.
>
> After "reading" the text this way, the children answered questions about it.
>
> "What does Sally have?" Verna asked.
>
> "A fish," they replied.
>
> "What color is her fish?"
>
> "Red."
>
> "Did Sally spill the chips?"
>
> "Yes."
>
> "Did the cat eat the chips?"
>
> "Yes."

32 While the content of this lesson seems incongruous, I know, its form and conduct fit the Meadow Brook model perfectly. Precise recall and yeses are all that the questions demand. Even the last question, while not covered in the "reading," requires recognition of only what happens in the picture.

33 What happened in Meadow Brook School that day—and what would happen in the eight school years to follow—reinforced, extended, and rarely contradicted what Eli already knew about literacy. Reading and writing at school allowed him to further affiliate and identify himself with and within his social group. While his teacher occasionally gave direct instructions, those instructions tended to be for activities never before seen or experienced; otherwise, Eli and Mary knew to follow the behavioral and attitudinal lead of the older children and to look to them for assistance and support, just as they looked to the teacher. In other words, reading

the school world came as naturally to these children as reading the world anywhere else, and the message in both texts was emphatically the same.

34   Most important here, however, may be the remarkable substantive coherence that Meadow Brook School provided, a coherence that precluded any conflict over what, how, or even whether to read and write. Eli's experience as a Fisher had taught him that reading comes in many forms—secular and religious, silent and oral, individual and communal—and they all count. Through his at-home experience, Eli also had learned which other, more specific, less obvious abilities count as reading in his world. He had learned to value at least four significant abilities: (1) the ability to select and manage texts, to be able to find his mother's letter in *Die Botschaft* or to find a particular verse in the Bible; (2) the ability to empathize with people in texts and to discern the implicit lessons their experiences teach: to empathize with Lambert the lion who taught the possibility of peaceful coexistence, and to empathize with the Anabaptist martyrs, who taught the rightness of dying for one's faith; (3) the ability to accurately recall what was read, to remember stories, riddles, and jokes or to memorize Bible and hymn verses; and (4) the ability to synthesize what is read in a single text with what is already known or to synthesize information across texts in Amish-appropriate ways.

35   When Eli got to school, he found a similar definition of reading in operation. He and Mary were helped to select and manage text. Their attention was directed toward what mattered in the text and away from what did not. They were helped to discover the single right answer to every question. They had only to recall information without interpreting or extending it in any significant way. And they were expected to empathize with the people in Verna's lunchtime oral reading without questioning or hypothesizing about what had happened or what would happen next.

36   Similarly, before Eli went to school, he knew what counted as writing in his world, just as he knew what counted as reading. He learned at home that being able to write means being able to encode, to copy, to follow format, to choose content, and to list. And, when he arrived at school, this same definition, these same abilities, were all that mattered there, too.

37   While the dimensions of reading and writing that count at Meadow Brook and elsewhere in Eli's life seem little different from those that count in mainstream situations—a terrifying fact, I would suggest—it is important to recognize that several mainstream-valued skills are completely absent from the Amish world as I've experienced it. Critical reading—individual analysis and interpretation—of the sort considered particularly important by most people who are mainstream-educated or mainstream educators is not valued by the Amish because of its potentially divisive, counterproductive power.

38   Literary appreciation, too, is both irrelevant and absent because the study of text-as-object is moot. How a writer enables a reader to empathize with his characters doesn't matter; only the ability to empathize matters. Text, whether biblical or secular, is perceived not as an object but as a force acting in the world, and it is the impact of that force that counts.

39   When it comes to writing, the existing Amish definition also differs in what is absent, rather than what is present. While grammar, spelling, and punctuation do count for the Old Order, they do so only to the extent that word order, words, and punctuation must allow readers to read—that is, to recognize and make sense of their reading. If a reader readily understands the intention of an adjective used as an adverb, a singular verb following a plural noun, a sentence fragment, or a compound verb containing a misplaced comma, the Amish do not see these as errors warranting attention, despite the fact that an outside reader may.

40   Equally irrelevant in Old Order schools is the third-person formal essay—the ominous five-paragraph theme—so prevalent in mainstream classrooms. Amish children never learn to write this kind of composition, not because they are not college-bound but because the third-person-singular point of view assumed by an individual writer is foreign to this first-person-plural society; thesis statements, topic sentences, and concepts like coherence, unity, and emphasis are similarly alien.

41   One final distinction separates the Amish definition of literacy from that of many mainstream definitions: the absence of originality as a desirable feature. Not only do community constraints limit the number of appropriate topics and forms an Amish writer may use, but original approaches to or applications of those topics and forms is implicitly discouraged by the similarly of models and assignments and by the absence of fiction as an appropriate personal genre. All aspects of community life reward uniformity; while writing provides an outlet for individual expression and identification, singular creativity stays within community norms.

42   For Eli Fisher, Jr., then, the definition of literacy he learned at home was consistent with the one he found at school, though it differed in several important ways from those of most MLA members, for example. Yet for Eli, as for Friere, "deciphering the word flowed naturally from reading the immediate world" (7). From reading his world, this six-year-old derived a complete implicit definition that told him what literacy is and whether literacy matters. I can't help but wonder, however, what would have happened had Eli gone to school and been told, explicitly or through more powerful behaviors, that he really didn't know what counted as reading and writing, that his reading and writing were not real but other unknown or alien varieties were. What would have happened had his quiet imitative behavior made him invisible in the classroom or, worse yet, made his teacher assume that he was withdrawn, problematic, or less than bright? What if his work were devalued because it was obviously copied or just unoriginal? What if he had been called on to perform individually in front of the class, to stand up and stand out? Or what if he had been asked to discuss private issues in public? Or to evaluate what he read?

43   Had any of these things happened, I suspect that Eli would have had to make some difficult choices that would have amounted to choosing between what he had learned and learned to value at home and what he seemed expected to learn at school. To conform to his teacher's demands and values, he would have had to devalue or disavow those of his parents—a demand that public schools seem to make frequently of children from cultural or socioeconomic groups differing from those of their teachers or their schools, a demand that seems unfair, uncalled for, and unnecessary, not to mention counterproductive and destructive.

44   Eli Fisher's experience suggests, therefore, that those of us who deal with children unlike ourselves need to see our classrooms and our students differently from the way we may have seen them in the past. We need to realize that students, even first-graders, have been reading the world—if not the word—for at least five, six, or seven years; they come to school not devoid of knowledge and values but with a clear sense of what their world demands and requires, including what, whether, and how to read and write, though their understanding may differ significantly from our own. We need to realize that our role may not be to prepare our students to enter mainstream society but, rather, to help them see what mainstream society offers and what it takes away, what they may gain by assimilating and what they may lose in that process. Through understanding their worlds, their definitions of literacy, and their dilemmas, not only will we better help them make important literacy-related decisions, but we will better help ourselves to do the same.

Works Cited

Freire, Paulo. "The Importance of the Act of Reading." *Journal of Education* Winter 1983: 5-10.

Heath, Shirley Brice. *Ways with Words: Language, Life, and Work in Communities and Classrooms.* Cambridge: Cambridge UP, 1983.

Taylor, Denny. *Family Literacy.* Portsmouth: Heinemann, 1983.

Wells, Gordon. *The Meaning Makers.* Portsmouth: Heinemann, 1986.

Questions for Discussion and Reflection

1 What are some of the ways Eli, Jr. and his family's understandings of reading and writing seem to differ from those of what Fishman calls "mainstream society"?

2 What are some of the various encounters with reading and writing Eli, Jr. has at home and in school? Do any of these seem familiar to you? Why or why not?

3 In paragraph 1 (p. 11), Fishman writes of Eli's preschool literacy experiences that "what he learned went far beyond academic readiness lessons. More important, Eli learned that literacy is a force in the world—his world—and it is a force that imparts power to all who wield it." What do you think Fishman means by this? How was literacy a "force" in Eli's world, and how has it been a force in yours?

4 Near the end of her article, Fishman offers a critique of what public schools demand in terms of student conformity as regards to literacy. In your own words, what is Fishman trying to say here? Do you agree with her argument? Why or why not?

Activities for Further Exploration

1 Fishman describes a number of Eli's encounters with reading and writing at home and school in careful detail. Use this as a model for a description of one of your own early encounters with literacy.

2 The first couple of pages of Fishman's article portray the Fishers at home, highlighting several occasions of reading and writing that are integrated naturally into the family's evening activities. One takeaway from these descriptions is that we are often surrounded by reading and writing (and opportunities to learn about reading and writing) without even really thinking about them. With that in mind, conduct some of your own research into **literate activity** happening around you. Take a notebook with you to some place where you can (unobtrusively) sit back and observe. Make note of all of the ways you see reading and writing—in any form—being used. Try to record specific details: what are people saying? What do the texts they are using look like? What might an outsider to this activity be surprised or confused by? Then, write up your notes in a one or two page descriptive account that shares what you observed and what you found most interesting.

What Can First-Year Composition at UCF Look Like?

To give you a sense of what the writing and research in your composition classes might look like, we have included in this section two articles (and a related **annotated bibliography**) written by UCF students. These two students—Madeline Halvey and Isaac Kyle—wrote these pieces in their composition classes and were then selected for publication in *Stylus: A Journal of First-Year Writing*, UCF's own journal of first-year student writing (see http://writingandrhetoric.cah.ucf.edu/stylus/). They demonstrate the outstanding work student writers and researchers are capable of, and we hope they serve as inspiration for your own investigations into writing.

"Simple Forms of Dance and Movement Literacy"

by Madeline Halvey

Halvey, Madeline. "Simple Forms of Dance and Movement Literacy." *Stylus: A Journal of First-Year Writing* 6.1 (2015): 28-36. Web. 5 Jan. 2015.

Madeline Halvey was a sophomore at UCF when she produced the following article in Kevin Roozen's Composition II class. This article later went on to win 2nd Runner-Up for the 2015 President John C. Hitt Prize for Excellence in First-Year Writing. If you have already read Andrea R. Fishman's "Becoming Literate: A Lesson from the Amish" on p. 6, you can think of Halvey's article as a sort of continuation of that work. Like Fishman, Halvey is interested in how literacy gets used in the real world. In particular, Halvey wants to find out how what she calls "simple" literate activities contribute to a dancer's success.

1   "Okay, that was a good run. Now go grab your notebooks and come sit over here for corrections." These directions are nothing new to dancers at the Cambridge School of Ballet—in fact, this scene happens at almost every rehearsal, especially during the few weeks before a performance. What the students are about to do is not what most expect out of a dance class: they are going to write down what they did wrong and what they need to improve.

2   For centuries, dance forms such as ballet have been studied through imitation and visual learning techniques. Thus, reading and writing are not often readily associated with this type of physical movement. However, as established above, there are small, yet important forms of literate activity within the dance realm that profoundly impact the learning processes of dance instruction. Such evidence of dance literacy has been studied over the past thirty years through debates over what is considered proper dance pedagogy (Cooper; Davenport and Forbes; Forbes) and how movement literacy is applied in specific, real-life situations (Perry; Phillips). Over the past two years, this debate has focused on digitizing dance education (Alvarez; Lehoux; Skjulstad and Morrison; Sutil).

3   Intriguingly, the complex forms of dance literacy have been studied to a greater extent than its simpler counterparts. Cooper argues that analyzing and describing dance movement through the use of essays and extended literary works benefits a dancer's literacy of movement. She concludes from her studies as a college-level dance instructor that together, dancing and writing can enhance a dancer but only when that writing is fully "embodied," or has much depth and analysis (Cooper 53). Davenport and Forbes similarly discuss the "use of dance to teach grammar, punctuation, phrasing, and shape in written language" (292). Cheryl Forbes, a language professor who enrolled in Donna Davenport's dance class, was especially intrigued by the connection between body movement and literacy, claiming that "most of us need to be instructed to connect with our bodies as we write" (302). In this case, both scholars put to practice the "embodied" writing Cooper advocates—

they use feelings of body movement from dance as their foundation to connect themselves to the writing experience (Davenport and Forbes).

4 Lehoux claims that the best understanding of dance movement is through notation systems, which describe the movement of the body through symbols on a staff, and act as a form of documentation for choreography. The significance of these systems is their adaptability to the digital times, as well as their ability to "contribute to a richer dance heritage" (Lehoux 154). Sutil, too, argues that a specific notation system, Labanotation, is particularly beneficial as a form of dance literacy in that it molds thinking and dance analysis together. However, notation systems are learned solely through years of training—exemplifying the complexity of this form of dance literacy.

5 What most dance and literacy scholars have not discussed is the technique of documenting dance corrections and choreography pertaining to specific dance instruction. In fact, all leading dance literacy scholars previously mentioned have lacked incorporation of the simplest forms of dance literacy into their studies. One scholar has come close. Newkirk broke ground in studies of children's artwork, claiming that they were fully functioning forms of literacy, despite the lack of actual text. Though it doesn't pertain to dance specifically, Newkirk's studies of pictorial literacy complement the findings from one of the cases in my following study, which incorporates child-like drawings and symbols as a form of her dance literacy.

6 The purpose of this study is to explore the literacy techniques found in a specific case study where literate dance activity revolves primarily around writing choreography and corrections, and to compare this case study to the pedagogy of a lower-level college dance class. As a foundation for my research in this area of study, I would like to look further into the literate form of dance movement, and pose the following questions: do literate forms of dance have to be fully comprehensive in order to serve a purpose in the dance realm? Can simpler forms of movement literacy be those that are most beneficial for dance pedagogy?

Methods

7 In this data analysis, I focused on two case studies: one of a dance instructor named Briana and another of a college-level ballet class. My data from Briana is compiled from her answers to a twelve-question e-mail interview I sent her, which asked general questions about her literate activities for any movement-based part of her life. I've known Briana since she first started teaching dance, and I have been a student in her Jazz class for the past three years. Over the past few months, I've had the privilege of observing her Jazz class and used this time to assess her teaching methods, incorporating what Prior calls "participant observation" (519). For instance, in the beginning of the dance year (August-September), I was a participant in the Jazz class, learning with the rest of the students; once she began to teach choreography for the studio's Nutcracker performance in November, I took on more of an observer's role. More recently, I spent my time in her Jazz class writing corrections for the dance her students are practicing to perform; this is something Briana asked me to do, as she needed another "set of eyes" to watch for mistakes in the choreography of her piece. To fully integrate "data from multiple sources," I've supplemented the interview and observations with pictures of Briana's literate activity in dance (Prior 519).

8   Other data I have collected is from a college-level ballet class I enrolled in during the Fall 2014 semester. This class provided sufficient data from many sources. First, I e-mailed this course's instructor, Kris, the same twelve-question interview that I sent to Briana. This gave me a general understanding of the movement-based literacy activities Kris practices. Next, I compiled the class syllabus, assignments, and required texts that make up most of the literate activities within the class. By doing this, I was able to implement the process of "tracing a series of texts" (Prior 500). Finally, my data analysis includes my personal experience in Kris' class and how her incorporation of literate activity affected my role as a student.

9   From their interviews, my observations, and my experiences in both Briana's and Kris' dance classes, I will compare the movement-based literate activities of each class.

Case Study: Briana

10   Now in her early twenties, Briana Hofer has been dancing since she was seven. She is a recent graduate of the University of Central Florida, where she studied Sports and Exercise Science. Since becoming a jazz, pointe, and ballet instructor at Cambridge School of Ballet (CSO) in Orlando, Florida four years ago, Briana added a literate form of dance to her movement studies. In part, this is due to CSO's policy of requiring upper-level dance students to write in a notebook the dance corrections that they were given verbally. Although Briana's role as a dance instructor requires her to incorporate forms of dance movement literacy, she also chooses to incorporate literate activity into other kinesthetic activities in her life (namely, workouts). In this case study, I look specifically at Briana's literacy as a dance instructor.

Role of Dance Instructor: Choreography and Corrections

11   Briana's main dance literate activity as an instructor is her written choreography and corrections. Briana writes choreography about three times a year and brings her written choreography texts in a binder to every class she teaches. Most of her pages are filled with text from top to bottom. Briana writes cast lists, movement words, positions, and "other things [she] wants to emphasize"—all of which are supplemented by small "drawings" to visually supplement her text. Figure 1-1 is an example of these drawings. In this picture, the dots represent dancers and the arrows establish the dancers' movements across the stage. Briana tends to write in different colored inks to separate sections of choreography. As seen in Figure 1-2, her "chunks" of choreography are similar to paragraphs of an essay—they mark

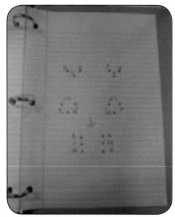

Figure 1-1: A page from Briana's dance binder showing some of her drawings.

when movement pauses or changes slightly in style or movement. Briana's writing style helps her define parts of the piece where the dancers are in new spots or where the actual choreography differs from the previous choreography (on this specific page the "chunks" differentiate between the "fighting" and "dancing" parts of the piece).

12   During rehearsal of her choreography, Briana watches her class perform the piece and takes note of the dancers' movements on a scrap piece of paper. These notes are called "corrections," or movements the dancers can specifically improve upon. When the performance is finished, Briana verbalizes the corrections she wrote out, often exemplifying certain steps or styles of the choreography that she wants her dancers to emphasize in the piece. Briana mentioned in her interview that she only rereads her written corrections aloud one time before crossing them off and never looking at them again. She goes through this whole process each time the piece is rehearsed.

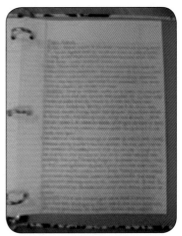

Figure 1-2: A page from Briana's dance binder showing some of her written choreography for her piece "Fight Scene."

Uses of Digital (or Technology-Based) Dance Literacy

13   Though she did not mention it in her interview, Briana uses technology as she writes choreography. Most ballet variations are age-old: choreography for specific pieces has been set years ago and remains virtually intact to this day (this is called Petipa, after French choreographer Marius Petipa). CSO Ballet uses similar theories for their performances. That is, Briana watches videos of past performances of "The Nutcracker," which is the choreography she is currently teaching, and writes down the movements of the dancers. She then adds her own "flair" of movements to the choreography without vastly changing what was already set. Briana writes down past choreography and changes it only in ways that benefit her dancers' physical abilities. For instance, Briana changed a set of eight count movement in the middle of her "fight scene" Nutcracker piece (Figure 2) because her dancers had improved since they last performed this piece and they needed to be challenged with more difficult choreography.

14   Not only does Briana watch dance videos to learn ballet choreography, but she also shows her class the videos she takes choreography from so that they can understand how the movement works. She points out what she likes in the video, what she is going to change about the video's choreography, and how the dancers can improve their own performance of this particular choreography. In doing this, Briana teaches her students how to learn from other dancers.

15   Briana reported that she keeps herself up-to-date about the dance world by reading what she refers to as "random articles" online pertaining to dance or working out. When she needs fresh ideas for teaching a ballet class, Briana refers to 100 Lessons in Classical Ballet by Vera S. Kostrovitskaya. For instance, if Briana is having a difficult time creating a combination for her ballet class to do at barre, she might refer to one of these texts for inspiration.

16   As an additional literate activity, Briana started a workout journal around the same time she began documenting dance. Briana's workout journals are not related

to dance, but they do document literate activity in her other high-priority kinesthetic activity: exercising. Briana writes in her workout journal about five times a week, documenting what workout movements she's done that day and which ones she has deemed "especially good" or "most beneficial." Unlike her dance corrections, Briana reads back over her workout journal multiple times. Even though she writes in her workout journal at home, Briana brings it wherever and whenever she works out. She has filled many workout journals throughout the past four years.

Summary

17   Briana has taught herself to use reading, writing, and drawing as forms of literate dance activity for her occupation as a dance instructor. She has learned to apply each type of activity to her students, her job, and her personal reflection. From this, I can conclude that Briana has fully integrated the two worlds of literate and kinesthetic activities into one interrelated set of processes.

Case Study: Kris

18   Kristina "Kris" Stevens is a ballet instructor at both Valencia College in Orlando, Florida and Rollins College in Winter Park, Florida. She has been a part of many dance companies, worked as a dancer/actor for Disney and received a degree in Dance from Valencia College. Kris' literate movement activity revolves solely around dance. In this case study, I will analyze all forms of Kris' literate dance activity.

Role of Dance Instructor: Assignments and Exams

19   As a college professor of dance, Kris writes lesson plans and choreography for students a couple of times each week. A visual learner, Kris says writing down her choreography or lessons helps her remember and clarify information, particularly which teaching methods and choreography work best or are most enjoyable. She keeps all of her class lessons and past choreography in both notebooks and computer files, and she will often reread her writings to reuse the information in future classes.

20   As her Ballet 1 class is a college course, Kris has also written a class syllabus that explains expectations, grading policies, assignments, required materials, and the "Valencia Department of Dance Writing Principles." The syllabus requires two textbooks for student use: The Technical Manual and Dictionary of Classical Ballet by Gail Grant and Ballet Basics by Sandra Noll Hammond. Both of these include written descriptions of ballet terms, forms, and movements, as well as pictures and figures that demonstrate the movement. Care of the body and proper dance etiquette also make up a few chapters in the Hammond textbook. During class, focus is on the five basic ballet positions and the eight positions of the body. Kris has her students first look at the picture of a certain form or movement, then read the text describing the movement, and then do the movement themselves.

21   The syllabus also outlines the dates and explanations for exams and assignments throughout the semester, which includes a written midterm, seventy-six note cards for studying, an essay reviewing a dance performance that her students must attend, and a dance presentation final.

22   Kris' pedagogy puts heavy emphasis on writing correct ballet terms. One assignment we did before the midterm, for example, encompassed memorization of seventy-six fundamental ballet terms by writing their definition and pronunciation on the front and back of a note card (Figure 1-3). In this way, my fellow classmates and I were able to really learn the ballet terms, which I found helpful for both the midterm and barre exercises in class.

Figure 1-3: One of the notecards cards I made for Kris' "notecard card assignment."

23   As another literate dance activity, Kris writes difficult or certain barre exercises on the whiteboard in the dance room at the end of class. Her students are required to write these combinations down, work on them at home using the written form for reference, and then perform the same exercise with improvement during the next class. To provide some guided study, Kris has her students read certain chapters of the textbooks that demonstrate specific movements. Figure 1-4 includes a few of my combination entries and notes from the months of August and September.

24   Finally, all dance classes at Valencia require students to write a four- to five-page essay about the Choreographers' Showcase Dance Performance, which all dance students are required to attend. The essay analyzes and critiques a minimum of four dance pieces that were part of the Choreographers' Showcase. The essay has specific requirements (e.g. MLA formatting) that are listed on the assignment page in Blackboard. Different from all of her other assignments, this activity is Kris' most complex.

Uses of Digital (or Technology-Based) Dance Literacy

25   This ballet course also includes an online component called Blackboard. Blackboard is a website used by Valencia College where Kris can post files, assignments, and messages for her students. Currently, she posts the

Figure 1-4: A page from my dance notebook for Kris' class showing certain combinations we learned and homework she assigned.

syllabus, a list of ballet terms and definitions, music from a dance piece the class is performing, the essay assignment guidelines, and a few miscellaneous documents about dance and the body.

26   Kris allows her students to use cell phones, laptops, and/or other devices to record her teaching of new barre combinations or choreography during class time. She then has the students post their recordings on Blackboard so that all the students in the class may see them.

27   Kris reads many pieces of literature regarding dance (biographies, programs for concerts, "how-to" articles, pedagogy essays and books, and reviews) mainly for her own enjoyment in learning about the topic. Recently, she had her class read a blog from another dance instructor that was written to motivate students to work harder.

Summary

28   Kris learned to be literate in dance from both her degree in dance as well as her many years teaching the subject at the college-level (which requires texts, grades, and policies to qualify as a credit course). Kris applies many different forms of dance literacy to her course, involving both simple and complex literate activity. In my own experience, I found the simpler forms to be most helpful in my navigation through the course. That being said, I have yet to reach the most complex literate activity of the course—the essay.

29   Like Briana, Kris has integrated the two worlds of dance and literacy.

Comparison: Briana and Kris

30   Upon enrolling in Kris' Ballet 1 class at Valencia College, I found that the way Kris teaches is similar to Briana in some aspects but includes more structure and maintains a different focus. Similarities occur in the way both instructors write choreography in a binder that they bring with them and look over during class. Both seem to find inspiration for their dance classes by reading recent dance literature, such as news articles about dance and books entailing proper dance technique. Kris recently had her students read a blog post from a dance instructor talking about motivation in ballet; this is much like the articles about dance Briana reads on the Internet. Both use textbooks about ballet fundamentals to help with their barre combinations for ballet class: Kris reads from Ballet Basics by Sandra Noll Hammond while Briana chooses 100 Lessons in Classical Ballet by Vera S. Kostrovitskaya.

31   Despite these parallels, Kris' dance pedagogy is much more structured than Briana's. Whereas Briana has her students write their dance corrections in their own personal styles, Kris has her students write the movement combination they are doing in correct French. This may have to do more with the mental and physical level of dance students each instructor has contact with: Kris works with students primarily new to the dance realm, while Briana has been working with most of the same girls since her first year teaching. Thus, Kris' form of dance literacy requiring text is most beneficial for her beginner students, while Briana's lack thereof still effectively incorporates a form of dance literacy that is best for her more advanced dancers.

Discussion

32   In her studies of dance, Cooper found that "the creative and compositional processes involved in dance-making and writing are complementary" (53). This concept coincides with what many literacy scholars have to say about literacy across two or more discourse communities. For example, Newkirk's study focuses on the literacy of children's drawings. He analyzed students' artwork and found that "drawing can help develop perceptual ability—the ability to make refined observations, which is useful for more than artwork" (104). While Briana's dance literacy (specifically her written choreography and corrections) may not be anything like the literate activity that Newkirk examined, it exemplifies his idea that these simple forms of literacy are useful in multiple genres and situations. This can be seen in Briana's beginning to write her workout journals around the same time her new occupation as a dance instructor required her to be literate in dance. Briana is not only improving her ability to be literate, but she is building her ability to observe and analyze her own processes and performance in dance and exercise.

33   Dance literacy studies like Cooper's, however, fail to discuss the simple forms of dance literacy that we see in Briana's work. Cooper tells us that dancing and writing can together enhance a dancer, but only when that writing is fully "embodied" (54). That is, based on her successful student analyses of dance movement, Cooper believes deep explanation of movement that gives "a real sense of dance as a sensual and corporeal experience" is the best way to experience dance literacy (59). I disagree, noting that Briana's simple system of dance literacy invokes personal growth and reflects her maturity in the dance realm. She has not only learned to be effective with her literacy techniques in regards to her work as a dance instructor, but she also applies these reflection techniques to her personal workout experience. Likewise, Briana provides an example for her dance students to be equally literate in the art of dance.

34   Similar to Cooper, Davenport and Forbes' campaign for extended analysis of dance literacy fails to explain Briana's literate dance activities. According to Davenport and Forbes, both writers and dancers can benefit from experiencing the mind-body connection. Specifically, dancers would do well to think of their movement as grammar: colons, semicolons, and punctuation that put "flow" in their "kinesthetic experience" (Davenport and Forbes 300). Davenport incorporated literacy in her dance classes by having the students do an activity that Forbes fashioned for her writing students: to rewrite (or, in this case, re-choreograph) different endings to a movement piece in order to find the best one possible (300). While this form of dance literacy is arguably beneficial to dance pedagogy, it doesn't encompass all beneficial techniques in the dance instruction practice. Briana teaches her students to write down the choreography they learn as well as the corrections they are given. My own college-level ballet class also includes writing specific choreography or combinations. Both instances provide a foundation to grow as a dancer. These simple forms of dance literacy improve students' "synthesis of knowledge, and retention of new information" as they learn to understand the basics of their movement (Davenport and Forbes 300).

35   In a wholly disparate form of dance literacy, Lehoux affirms that "notation systems are essential to the description of movement" (154). Sutil agrees, specifying

that Labanotation "has found a new readership in digital dance contexts" of this century (161). In simpler terms, both scholars make the claim that these complex forms of movement documentation (similar to music scores) are advantageous to dance literacy. While intrigued by the idea of using staff and symbols as representations of body movement and pieces of choreography, I can't help but disagree as I find these systems unnecessarily complex. Briana cohesively documents her choreography using language she understands best and is effectively able to teach her movements this way. More than that, Briana develops most of her choreography from past performances that she and her dancers watch on video. I argue that learning from choreography documented this way (video and written) is much more effective in helping dancers develop specific style or flair to their dance. As she shows her dancers a video of choreography, Briana points out certain parts that can be improved, changed, or incorporated into her dancers' movement of the piece. While notation systems may contribute to "richer dance heritage" in the long run, they only apply to students who are trained in the system (Lehoux 154). Primitive forms of dance literacy, however, can be universally understood and applied.

36   Over the years, dance has become more of a literate activity than ever before, even though I argue that the most beneficial dance movement literate activities are those in the simple form. From this perspective, the understanding we might want to more readily incorporate into dance pedagogy is simply the ways students learn and are taught to do movement pieces—as well as the way choreographers or dance instructors develop, teach, and improve those pieces—by simple forms of writing and watching other dancers. From my observations during this study, there are many ways dancers learn choreography and take corrections; perhaps applications of many different pedagogical practices of dance instruction (a mix of simple and complex forms) could result in a more approachable and comprehensive design of dance instruction.

Works Cited

Alvarez, Inma. "High Aspirations: Transforming Dance Students from Print Consumers to Digital Producers." *Nottingham OER* 2013. Spec. issue of *Journal of Interactive Media in Education* (2013): n. pag. Web. 12 Sept. 2014.

Cooper, Debra. "Embodied Writing: A Tool for Teaching and Writing in Dance." *Journal of Dance Education* 11.2 (2011): 53-59. SPORTDiscus. Web. 12 Sept. 2014.

Davenport, Donna R., and Cheryl A. Forbes. "Writing Movement/Dancing Words: A Collaborative Pedagogy." *Education* 118.2 (1997): 292-302. *Professional Development Collection.* Web. 11 Sept. 2014.

Forbes, Cheryl. "Writing the Body: An Experiment in Material Rhetoric." *Rhetoric Review* 19.1-2 (2000): 60-72. JSTOR. Web. 12 Sept. 2014.

Lehoux, Natalie. "Dance Literacy and Digital Media: Negotiating Past, Present, and Future Representations of Movement." *International Journal of Performance Arts & Digital Media* 9.1 (2013): 153-74. *International Bibliography of Theatre & Dance.* Web. 11 Sept. 2014.

Newkirk, Thomas. Draw Me a Word, Write Me a Picture." *More Than Stories: The Range of Children's Writing.* Portsmouth, NH: Heinemann, 1989. 35-66. Rpt. in Wardle and Downs 76-104. Print.

Perry, Kathryn. "The Movement of Composition: Dance and Writing." *Kairos: A Journal of Rhetoric, Technology, and Pedagogy* 17.1 (2012): n. pag. Web. 12 Sept. 2014.

Phillips, Susan A. "Crip Walk, Villain Dance, Pueblo Stroll: The Embodiment of Writing in African American Gang Dance." *Anthropological Quarterly* 82.1 (2009): 69-97. JSTOR. Web. 10 Sept. 2014.

Prior, Paul. "Tracing Process: How Texts Come Into Being." *What Writing Does and How It Does It.* Ed. Charles Bazerman and Paul Prior. Mahwah, NJ: Lawrence Erlbaum, 2004. 167-200. Rpt. in Wardle and Downs 492-525. Print.

Skjulstad, Synne, and Andrew Morrison. "Movement in the Interface." *Computers and Composition* 22.4 (2005): 413-33. ScienceDirect. Web. 12 Sept. 2014.

Sutil, Nicolas Salazar. "Laban's Choreosophical Model: Movement Visualisation Analysis and the Graphic Media Approach to Dance Studies. *Dance Research* 30.2 (2012): 147-68. *International Bibliography of Theatre & Dance.* Web. 12 Sept. 2014.

Wardle, Elizabeth, and Doug Downs, eds. *Writing about Writing: A College Reader.* 2nd ed. Boston: Bedford/St. Martins, 2014. Print.

Questions for Discussion and Reflection

❶ What does Halvey seem to mean by "literate activity"? Can you think of examples of literate activities in your own life?

❷ What methods did Halvey employ here? How did she investigate the connection between writing and dance classes? Why do you think these methods were appropriate given what she set out to learn? (to learn more about the methods available to writing researchers—including you—see *Chapter 2 p. 54*)

❸ How does Halvey use secondary research (i.e. sources) in this article? Where do they appear? What ideas does she seem to get from these sources? How does she contrast her study with previous research? In other words, what does Halvey see herself as adding to the ongoing conversation about these subjects?

❹ Halvey references researcher Thomas Newkirk to make the point that "Newkirk broke ground in studies of children's artwork, claiming that they were fully functioning forms of literacy, despite the lack of actual text" *(p. 19, paragraph 5)*. What do you think of this claim? What might be the implications of considering literacy as more than just reading or writing text with letters (what writing researchers sometimes call "alphabetic" text)?

Activities for Further Exploration

❶ One of the things we like about Halvey's article is how she is able to find and examine the literate activity in a context (dance class) in which we might not expect there to be much reading and writing. Try this out for yourself. Make a list of some of the different endeavors (think school, work, hobbies, and so forth) in which you participate on a daily or weekly basis. Then, jot down some of the literate activities associated with these endeavors. Finally, pick one literate activity that seems interesting or important to you and write a few paragraphs explaining that activity to someone unfamiliar with it. What goes into that literate activity? What do people engaging in that activity need to know? What might surprise an outsider to that activity? What might a researcher like Fishman or Halvey have to say about it? If you can, try to incorporate visuals to help explain your literate activity, like Halvey does in her article.

❷ Now, take your research a step further. Talk to someone else who participates in that same literate activity. What is their perception of the activity? How do they engage in it in ways that are similar to or different from how you do? Again, try to collect some data you can use (pictures, examples of texts) to help explain what you are finding to someone else. If you need some ideas for the sorts of questions to ask when interviewing someone, see *Chapter 2 p. 61*.

Annotated Bibliography for
"Simple Forms of Dance and Movement Literacy"
by Madeline Halvey

Madeline Halvey created the annotated bibliography below while compiling research for her article on dance and literacy in Kevin Roozen's Composition II class. An annotated bibliography is simply a bibliography (a list of sources referred to while researching) that includes an annotation (a brief summary and evaluation) for each source. Researchers use annotated bibliographies like this one to organize information as they collect it and to begin making connections between sources. You can see Halvey drawing these connections in the first paragraph of the brief introduction that precedes her lists of sources. Gathering and organizing research in this way also makes it easier for researchers to figure out what questions they want to pursue and address, which you see Halvey doing in the second paragraph of her introduction. For more information on gathering research of your own, see **Chapter 2**. For more information on citing research, see **Chapter 3**.

1   Dance forms, such as ballet, have been studied for centuries through imitation and visual learning techniques. Thus, reading and writing are not usually activities associated with this type of physical movement. However, there has been recent evidence of literacy within the dance realm. Within the past thirty years, there have been arguments of what is considered proper dance pedagogy (Cooper; Davenport and Forbes) and how movement literacy is applied in specific, real-life situations (Phillips); over the past two years, these arguments have turned to digitalizing dance education (Alvarez; Lehoux). What has not been discussed, though, is the technique of documenting dance corrections and choreography pertaining to specific dance instruction.

2   The purpose of this annotated bibliography is to provide background information on studies relating to dance and literacy while also exploring the lives, first-hand, of those who incorporate literacy into their dance studies. I would like to look further into the literate form of dance movement, and pose the following questions: does incorporating this type of writing technique into dance students' pedagogy at beginning levels of dance help in the development of a dancer? Can personal reflection in one type of movement be beneficial to other movement activities? Is personal reflection an effective way to improve group dance movement? Could learning proper dance movement language be key to improving the utilization of dance literature?

Primary Research

Hofer, Briana. Email Interview. 14 Sept. 2014. Briana is a ballet, Pointe, and jazz dance teacher at Cambridge School of Ballet in Orlando, Florida. She has been dancing competitively since she was seven, and received all of her dance training in the Orlando area. Briana is a UCF graduate of Sports and Exercise Science Strengthening and Conditioning track. I asked her twelve interview questions about her writing and reading activities that pertain to dance. In her interview, Briana states she did not start writing or reading in dance until she became a dance instructor four years ago. Since then, she has come to read and write in her other kinesthetic activities. For instance, she has many filled workout journals and writes in her current workout journal about five times a week. Briana taught herself how to write about dance; however, she does refer to *100 Lesson's in Classical Ballet* by Vera S. Kostrovitskaya, as well as online articles about workout or dance, as inspiration for new teaching methods or dance combination ideas. Finally, Briana writes choreography and corrections as part of her job as a dance instructor. She writes choreography three times a year, and she writes corrections every dance rehearsal (though once she has expressed a correction verbally to a dancer, she doesn't look back at her written correction). This interview with Briana poses the questions of whether teaching literate techniques in beginning dance classes will help in both dance movement and other kinesthetic activities in the future or as the activities progress to higher levels.

Judy, Chandra. Email Interview. 14 Sept. 2014. Judy is a ballet teacher at Cambridge School of Ballet in Orlando, Florida. She has a B.F.A with Honors in Choreography from Wright State University and has been a part of over five dance companies across the Eastern U.S. I asked her twelve interview questions about her writing and reading activities that pertain to dance. Judy's main literacies in dance include writing choreography and lesson plans for the classes she teaches. She writes her plans once a week and has been participating in these literate activities for over thirty years now. Judy keeps all her written materials regarding dance either in a binder that she takes with her to teach or in "easily assessable" files at her home. She writes strictly at home and always in English. Most importantly, Judy writes for many reasons: improvement of dancers, "edification of self-education," "artistic expression and beauty of movement through choreography," "time saving when referring back to choreography," and, what she deems most important, "Glory to God." This interview really shed light on writing corrections and choreography for interpersonal reasons—she doesn't just write for herself, but for a greater being, which she put much emphasis on in the interview.

Stevens, Kristina. Email Interview. 15 Sept. 2014. Kristina is a ballet instructor at both Valencia College in Orlando, Florida and Rollins College in Winter Park, Florida. She has been a part of many dance companies, worked as a dancer/actor for Disney, and finally received a degree in Dance from Valencia College. As a college professor of dance, Kristina writes a syllabus every semester as well as lesson plans, choreography, and corrections for students a couple times a week. She writes mainly at her workplace and does so in a combination of English and French language. A visual learner, Kristina says writing down her choreography or lessons helps her remember and clarify information—especially what teaching methods work best and choreography she particularly enjoyed. She keeps all of her class lessons and past choreography in both notebooks and computer files, and she will often reread her writings to reuse the information in future classes.

Kristina reads many pieces of literature regarding dance (biographies, programs for concerts, "how-to" articles, "pedagogy essay/books", and reviews) mainly for her own enjoyment of learning about the topic. This interview brought up the concept of college-level pedagogy of dance movement and how effective its use of literate activity is for beginning-level dancers.

Stevens, Kristina. "DAA 1200/1201 Syllabus." Print. 17 Sept. 2014. In this syllabus for her ballet one and two class at Valencia College in Orlando, Florida, Kristina emphasizes her classroom objectives and purpose. This syllabus documents the requirement of two texts: *The Technical Manual and Dictionary of Classical Ballet by Gail Grant* as well as *Ballet Basics* by Sandra Noll Hammond. Students are informed within the syllabus that they will be evaluated on not only their physical dance technique improvement over the course of the semester, but also on their final essay which is a critical writing assignment about a dance performance that students are required to attend. Other important aspects of this syllabus include: "Valencia Department of Dance [Writing] Principles," "Internet Research Statement," and "Grading Policy and Standards." This document is a vital piece of information for my study in that it is first-hand evidence of required literacy about dance movement.

Secondary Sources

Alvarez, Inma. "High Aspirations: Transforming Dance Students from Print Consumers to Digital Producers." Nottingham OER 2013. Spec. issue of Journal of Interactive Media in Education (2013): n. pag. Web. 12 Sept. 2014. In this article, Inma reports findings from a study in which a digital-based curriculum was incorporated into a Bachelor's of Dance program at a university. The technology created for this curriculum focused on e-learning materials for five classes as well as other numerous digital materials to assist in audio-visual learning. Inma found that, at first, students did not take to the digitalized version of dance education—they did not understand its connection to physical movement and they began to resist it. However, as the Dance Department became more technology-based, students began to see how using e-learning and other technologies bridged the gap between dance movement and dance literature, providing them with a more professional and experienced outlook on dance as a whole. This article is interesting in that it considers online learning as a supplement to face-to-face learning within dance pedagogy, thus broadening my scope of dance-related literacy.

Cooper, Debra. "Embodied Writing: A Tool for Teaching and Writing in Dance." Journal of Dance Education 11.2 (2011): 53-59. SPORTDiscus. Web. 12 Sept. 2014. This scholarly article focuses on incorporating vigorous writing activities into the curriculum of dance education. In her studies, Cooper created an introductory level undergraduate course where she designed a curriculum focused on compositional process of analyzing and describing dance movement—an activity she calls "embodied writing." Her method of research was to have students participate in classroom free-writes as well as an extensive writing assignment that acted as the final exam for the class. Using a thorough review and peer-editing process for this last and most important assignment, the author concluded that students successfully integrated her methods of dance composition in such a way that they were able to detail complete dance movement in descriptive prose (third person point of view) while also providing explanations for how it felt to complete dance movement (first person point of view). The author felt she had successfully completed her goal to bring awareness to student's complete compositional process, not only in dance, but in other discourse communities, as well. This focus of compositional processes about dance movement can be included in my study as an example of literate activity pertaining to dance movement that crosses two discourse communities.

Davenport, Donna R., and Cheryl A. Forbes. "Writing Movement/Dancing Words: A Collaborative Pedagogy." Education 118.2 (1997): 292-302. Professional Development Collection. Web. 11 Sept. 2014. In this collaborative journal article, Davenport and Forbes explore each other's departments and find pedagogical connections between the two. Both authors provide their own initial take on the exploration of the other's department—Davenport, a dancer, explores writing about dance; while Forbes, a writer, enrolls in a dance class to learn about movement. After their initial anecdotes, each author goes into detail about the connections they have made between dance movement and writing. They conclude that there are many similarities between the two departments. Davenport emphasized similarities in punctuation, vocabulary, and voice of dancers and writers, claiming that fusing the two pedagogies of dance and movement makes for a developed and experienced dancer. Likewise, Forbes articulates that her experience in dance has broadened her perspective about writing, particularly in regards to space, weight, and time. Together, these two authors conclude that while dance and writing are separate entities, they connect the mind and body in ways that promote an overall enhanced learning experience. I can include this unique collaboration in my article as a way to introduce the initial concept of writing about dance movement from both dancer and writer perspectives.

Lehoux, Natalie. "Dance Literacy and Digital Media: Negotiating Past, Present, and Future Representations of Movement." International Journal of Performance Arts & Digital Media 9.1 (2013): 153-74. International Bibliography of Theatre & Dance. Web. 11 Sept. 2014. This article takes a closer look at a historical notation system movement process that has been developing over the past thirty years. Lehoux defines the notation system as a symbolic representation of dance movement similar to recording music notes on a staff. She argues for a more developed use of notation systems in dance literature, emphasizing the need for notation system movement to be recorded digitally as a means to provide better access of dance records (such as choreography) for the dance community. In regards to my research on the topic of dance movement literacy, notation systems are a unique concept that provide more insight about recording techniques of dance movement.

Phillips, Susan A. "Crip Walk, Villain Dance, Pueblo Stroll: The Embodiment of Writing in African American Gang Dance." Anthropological Quarterly 82.1 (2009): 69-97. JSTOR. Web. 10 Sept. 2014. In this article, Phillips explores gang dance ceremonies involving double Dutch, dance movement, hand signals, and writing as a form of socially accepted expression. In her observations, this author found that gang-related literate activities were expressed in a form of movement called Crip Walk—a game in which members would skip rope and, at the same time, throw up hand signals or write memorials for loved ones in the dirt. Phillips also describes gang dances in which members of the African American communities will use specific dance step patterns as a way to sign, signal, or initial their gang affiliation. Phillips concludes that dance movement and writing make up an important part of gang-related communication. She infers that the body and the mind are never completely separable in these instances—they are incorporated in the distinction of gang literacy. This article is helpful to my research in that it exemplifies dance movement literacy across a discourse community that would otherwise not be related to what I had originally considered "dance movement."

Questions for Discussion and Reflection

❶ What purpose does each annotation seem to serve? If you are a reader unfamiliar with Halvey's research, what sort of information does each annotation include? What does an annotation tell you about the source? Try to link your discussion to one or two specific examples.

❷ What purpose does Halvey's brief introduction (the two paragraphs before her source lists) seem to serve? What does it do for you as a reader?

Activities for Further Exploration

❶ Look back at Halvey's finished article—it starts on *p. 18*—and search for two or three of the sources she writes about in this annotated bibliography. How are they being used? How is her writing in the finished article similar to or different from what she's written in these annotations?

❷ Next, look at the sources Halvey chose to include in her final article that are not in this annotated bibliography. Why do you think she chose to add these? What do they seem to do for her article?

❸ Find one of Halvey's secondary sources (they're all available electronically, either online or via the UCF Libraries website) and skim through it. How does the source compare to Halvey's annotation of it? What did Halvey choose to focus on in her annotation, and why do you think she chose to do so? Conversely, what did Halvey leave out, and why do you think she did so?

"Rhetorical Reflection on an Air Force IT Ad"
by Isaac Kyle

Kyle, Isaac. "Rhetorical Reflection on an Air Force IT Ad." *Stylus: A Journal of First-Year Writing* 6.1 (2015): 1-4. Web. 5 Jan. 2015.

Isaac Kyle was in his first year at UCF when he produced the following article in Vanessa Calkins' Composition I class during Fall 2014. Drawing on his experiences in the United States Air Force, Kyle created an advertisement to address what he perceived as a gap in the military's recruiting efforts: not enough young people know about the Air Force's career paths in information technology (IT). The article below describes the research and process that went into the creation of the ad, giving Kyle the opportunity to reflect on the many decisions he made along the way.

Kyle uses a number of terms you may not be familiar with (***activity system, exigence, social fact***) and uses what might be familiar terms in new ways (genre). When you encounter a term you do not know, take a minute to look it up. As you read, consider what these new terms add to Kyle's article. What do they allow him to say about the decisions he made while composing the ad, and what ideas do they lead you to think about as you reflect on your experiences as a writer?

1   Graduating high school or junior college can be a difficult experience for someone who has no idea what path they should take next. When I encountered this crossroad, I was certain that college was the next best option for me. However, financial deficiencies deterred me from my initial dream and led me down another course. It led to me joining the United States Air Force as a Network Technician. I've always had a knack for understanding how information technology worked; I just never assumed that I could possibly make a career out of it. While I was still in school, most options for students that were graduating were going to the local community college or finding a job in town. Military recruiters often visited our school, but none were from the Air Force. As a current Air Force veteran, I find it strange that the Air Force isn't marketing their opportunities in the information technology (IT) career field to all high school students. I recently created an advertisement that could be used to draw the attention of young adults that may be interested in the IT career field and how the Air Force can help them achieve their goals. The purpose of this essay is to reflect on some of the rhetorical choices I made while creating the ad (see Figure 1-5).

2   In preparation for creating the ad, I analyzed the career of a Network Technician as an activity system for research purposes. Kain and Wardle define an activity system as a group of people who share a common objective or motive over time (275). This analysis helped me understand how technicians interact among themselves and with the community surrounding them. It also gave me an in-depth look at what technicians do on a daily basis, and the purpose behind each task. This new perspective as an outsider opened my eyes to the many strengths and weaknesses within the activity system. A particular weakness that stood out to

Figure 1-5: The ad

me was the lack of diversity among network technicians. This new understanding helped me form an idea of creating an ad that could attract fresh and diverse recruits to join the Air Force as a communications troop. I decided that creating an advertisement would be the most successful method for me to depict this concept.

3   Understanding the exigence of the ad was simple. I wanted the ad to act as a recruiter and attract a young adult to join the Air Force. I specifically wanted the audience to gain interest in working in the communications side of this branch as well. In an interview with a former colleague of mine, James Sotiroff, I asked him what he would say to individuals if they wanted to pursue a career in IT for the Air Force. He responded by saying that the Air Force has a vast array of jobs within the IT career field and that an individual has many options. As a former network technician myself, I wholeheartedly agreed with him. However, I needed to find a way to portray that statement in the ad. I decided that using pictures showing current or former members doing technical work and training could promote the variety of IT jobs that an individual could be a part of within the Air Force. I tried using pictures that had members using tools in the activity system. Tools in activity systems are defined as physical objects and symbols that people use to accomplish the activity (Kain and Wardle 277). Nevertheless, the pictures by themselves may not be enough to understand what the ad is saying to an audience member. I added the question, "Interested in pursuing a career in IT?" to complement the pictures. I placed the question across the ad in order to portray what the photos represent: a career in IT. I also enlarged the question so the audience would read the text and see the multiple jobs that the Air Force could provide in the communications career field. In a last attempt to depict the exigence of the ad, I added a text box to promote the Air Force's capability of providing the best equipment and training to satisfy an interest in IT. I included the web address of the branch's website for the audience to further investigate this interest. However, the website I provided represents jobs across the entire Air Force. I used this address for individuals who might be interested in the Air Force for other careers, and not just one in

communications. After I completed the ad, I determined it would be best portrayed as a poster instead of a flyer. Posters tend to attract a multitude of people due to their large dimensions. However, a banner would be much too large and could possibly stretch the images being used. I wanted the audience to have a clear view of what was being advertised.

4   Determining the audience for this ad wasn't as easy as I would have hoped. In analyzing the activity system, I noted that most of the members of the system were white males, including my interviewee. I couldn't create the ad specifically targeting one demographic. In adding the pictures of the service members, I tried to include multiple ethnic groups and genders to convey that anyone can work in IT, not specifically white males. I did this because I wanted the intended audience— no matter their demographic—to feel that they could be a part of this organization. Keith Grant-Davie points out that rhetors may invite audiences to accept new identities for themselves, offering the readers a vision not of who they are but who they could be (356). I feel that this choice is the most successful aspect of the advertisement because of the way it speaks to the audience, as the audience may see themselves in the advertisement. I also applied a greyscale effect to each photo to depict that each member may be a different ethnicity or gender but they represent one team: the Air Force. In doing this, I wanted the audience to feel that each service member embodied the Air Force by being shown as one color.

5   Trying to connect to a wider audience was difficult in its own right. The biggest constraint I encountered while creating the ad was finding pictures of multiple ethnicities doing IT work for the Air Force. I believe this constraint could be the most problematic aspect of the advertisement. I was unable to find pictures that depicted various ethnicities, and more so for non-male ethnicities other than white. This constraint hindered my efforts to try and reach out to all ethnicities and genders who might be interested in joining the Air Force as an IT technician. Another constraint I encountered was trying to find a way to make the job of a technician seem enjoyable to someone who isn't necessarily interested in information technology. The Air Force has a multitude of jobs that garner interest from multiple perspectives. Jobs such as deactivating a bomb as an explosive ordinance technician or parachuting from an airplane to save wounded soldiers as a pararescueman can seem infinitely more attractive than fixing a backup server on a weekly basis. Charles Bazerman defined this concept as a social fact: "things people believe to be true, and therefore bear on how they define a situation" (368). I disputed this social fact by adding some pictures of the more tactical jobs an IT technician can encounter while in the Air Force. I felt that in viewing these pictures, the audience could view the IT career field as being more than fixing twenty dysfunctional keyboards in one day. I wanted the audience to—in the words of Haas and Flower—"construct meaning by building multifaceted, interwoven representations of knowledge" from the genre rather than a social fact (413).

6   After I finished creating the ad, I analyzed each aspect of the advertisement rhetorically. I determined my purpose for the advertisement, the intended audience, and the constraints I encountered while creating the piece. Afterwards, I tried to find an association between the ad and the activity system I had previously analyzed. The connection I found was that there are many significant roles that can

be filled by the Air Force's IT career field. I believe that my advertisement meets its goal by advertising the many IT jobs you can attain as a member of the U.S. Air Force. It also represents a diverse background of ethnicities and genders to convey that anyone can find their niche in communications and in the military.

Works Cited

Bazerman, Charles. "Speech Acts, Genres, and Activity Systems: How Texts Organize Activity and People." *What Writing Does and How It Does It: An Introduction to Analyzing Texts and Textual Practices*. Ed. Charles Bazerman and Paul Prior. London, Routledge: 2004. 309-39. Rpt. in Wardle and Downs 365-393. Print.

Grant-Davie, Keith. "Rhetorical Situations and Their Constituents." *Rhetoric Review* 15.2 (1997): 264-79. Rpt. in Wardle and Downs 347-64. Print.

Haas, Christina and Linda Flower. "Rhetorical Reading Strategies and the Construction of Meaning." *College Composition and Communication* (1988): 167-83. Rpt. in Wardle and Downs 411-426. Print.

Kain, Donna, and Elizabeth Wardle. "Activity Theory: An Introduction for the Writing Classroom." Wardle and Downs 273-83.

Wardle, Elizabeth, and Doug Downs, eds. *Writing about Writing: A College Reader*. 2nd ed. Boston: Bedford/St. Martins, 2014. Print.

Questions for Discussion and Reflection

❶ What are some of the challenges Kyle encountered while creating his ad? Can you relate to any of these?

❷ Look up the term "exigence." What does it mean in this context? What was Kyle's exigence in creating his ad? How does that compare to the exigencies you find yourself writing for on a regular basis?

❸ Kyle's reflections suggest the central role that audience played in his thinking about his writing. How do you think about audience when you write? Is it something you're aware of throughout the process, or only towards the end? How does your understanding of audience shape the decisions you make as a writer, if at all?

Activities for Further Exploration

❶ Use Kyle's article as a model for your own reflection on a text you've composed recently. This might be something you wrote for a class or a job, or it might be a visual text like Kyle's example. Try to remember as much as you can about the process that went into the creation of the text. What were you thinking about when you got started? How did you imagine your audience and what they would want to get out of the text? How long did it take you to create the text? What challenges did you encounter along the way? What decisions did you have to make? Write up your reflection in a one or two page report. If you can, include the actual text with your report, like Kyle did.

❷ Kyle argues that his ad was able to counter the "social fact" that audiences imagine other jobs in the Air Force as more exciting and attractive than IT positions. He quotes Charles Bazerman's definition of social facts as "things people believe to be true, and therefore bear on how they define a situation." Look up "social fact" online and see what you can find. What are some examples of social facts? How do you think this idea relates to writing? Can you think of any times you have had to write something that went against a social fact? What about times when your writing has been constrained by social facts?

Where Can You Get Support for Your Writing at UCF?

There are many resources at UCF you can take advantage of to support your writing, both during your time in composition classes and after. We've provided some information on these resources below.

University Writing Center

http://uwc.cah.ucf.edu

The University Writing Center (UWC) is for confident and struggling writers alike. The UWC offers individual writing support to students at all levels, from first-year to graduate, in all majors. The UWC is much more than a grammar lab. Instead, trained peer tutors assist at every stage of the writing process, from understanding the assignment, to drafting and organizing, to revision. Consultations are available face-to-face, online, and in small groups.

The UWC also provides a wealth of writing resources on the web, from style guides to handouts on professional writing, grammar, and punctuation.

The UWC has offices on the main UCF campus in Orlando as well as branches at the Rosen Library, Eastern Florida State College, and Daytona State College. Drop in, schedule an appointment online, or phone for an appointment. Information about hours, locations, and scheduling an appointment with the UWC can be found at http://uwc.cah.ucf.edu.

What are some things UWC tutors can help you do?

- Understand assignment requirements
- Develop ideas
- Plan and organize your writing
- Identify and address some key aspects of your writing for you to revise
- Learn to cite and document sources
- Practice strategies for proofreading and editing
- Learn to correct errors in grammar, punctuation, and mechanics

What can you do to the get the most out of a UWC consultation?

- Visit the UWC well before your assignment is due.

- Allow enough time to have multiple consultations (on different days) for big writing projects. You probably won't be able to discuss all aspects of your writing in just 30-45 minutes.
- You don't need to have a completed draft. Working with the UWC earlier in your writing process—even before you get started—can be just as useful.
- For long-term help, arrange a recurring weekly appointment to meet with the same tutor at the same time throughout the semester.
- If you're not sure how to handle a complicated assignment, or if you've got writer's block, those are good times to visit the UWC!

What should you bring to a UWC consultation?

- Your assignment requirements or guidelines for writing
- Your work—everything you've done so far
- Your notes, outline, sources—everything you've used to help you write
- Ideas, questions, and specific learning goals you'd like to accomplish

UCF Libraries

http://library.ucf.edu

Did you know that UCF has 14 libraries on multiple campuses? You may be familiar with the John C. Hitt Library in the center of the Orlando campus, but there are branch and regional libraries in many locations, including at the Rosen College, College of Medicine, Cocoa, Daytona Beach, and 9 other regional campuses. The UCF Libraries house almost 2 million items, including online books and journals accessible from anywhere in the world.

You can use the Libraries web page to search for items in any of the libraries' collections, and also search hundreds of databases for access to hundreds of thousands of articles, ebooks, and historical documents. Students simply log in to the Libraries web page with their NID, and all of this information is at their fingertips. Reference librarians are available at the Research & Information Desk and using the Ask Us service.

Useful Library Services for Composition Students

Ask Us

http://library.ucf.edu/ask/

The Ask Us service offers research assistance in person or via live chat, text message, email, or telephone. Reach a librarian when you really need one!

Interlibrary Loan (ILL)

http://library.ucf.edu/services/borrowing-from-other-libraries/

If there's an article or book that you need for your research, and the UCF Libraries don't have access, the Interlibrary Loan & Document Delivery Services (ILL/DDS) Department will get it for you! Interlibrary Loan borrows items from other libraries, and it's a free service for you. Students can request books, articles, and other materials through ILL by logging into their ILLiad account (which new users can create in a matter of minutes). Books are typically available in 7-10 business days, and articles are typically available to download within 3-5 business days.

Subject Librarians and UCF Research Guides

http://guides.ucf.edu

Did you know there is a Subject Librarian for your major? John Venecek is the librarian for Writing and Rhetoric, and there are librarians for each academic discipline at UCF from Accounting to Tourism.

The Research Guides are subject-specific guides created by Subject Librarians in their area. Each guide contains resources and collections that are important in a given discipline, and can serve as a useful entry point into your research, no matter the field.

Research Consultations

http://library.ucf.edu/help/schedule-an-appointment/

A Research Consultation is a one-on-one appointment with a librarian for extensive, in-depth research assistance. If you need extra help finding sources on a tough topic, you can schedule a session with your Subject Librarian.

Additional Online Resources

Stylus: A Journal of First-Year Writing

http://writingandrhetoric.cah.ucf.edu/stylus/

Since 2010, *Stylus: A Journal of First-Year Writing* has published two issues a year of outstanding writing from UCF's own first-year composition students. These articles can be all be found online at the journal's website, and might serve as inspiration for the writing and research you are doing in your own composition class. Look to what these past students have written for another perspective on a concept you've been talking about in class, ideas for how to investigate some aspect of your own writing, and models of how you might organize and present your own thinking.

Young Scholars in Writing

http://arc.lib.montana.edu/ojs/index.php/Young-Scholars-In-Writing/

As with *Stylus*, *Young Scholars in Writing: Undergraduate Research in Writing and Rhetoric* (*YSW*), a peer-reviewed journal for undergraduates, can provide inspiration and models for your own writing and research. The journal publishes research and theoretical articles from undergraduates on writing, writers, rhetoric, discourse, language, and related topics, so you should find the articles presented there highly relevant to the work you are doing in your composition class. There is also a "Spotlight on First-Year Writing" section in each issue that publishes work from students in first-year composition courses. All articles are accessible online. Visit the *YSW* website for details on submitting work for consideration.

CompPile

http://comppile.org/

CompPile is a database of publication information for books and articles relevant to writing studies. CompPile does not contain the texts themselves (though you can sometimes find a direct link), but many of the publications you discover in CompPile can be found in the UCF Libraries. This makes CompPile a useful first stop when researching subjects related to writing or rhetoric. Additionally, the WPA-CompPile research bibliographies (http://comppile.org/wpa/bibliographies/) provide quick overviews on a variety of writing- and literacy-related topics.

Purdue OWL

https://owl.english.purdue.edu/owl/

The Online Writing Lab (OWL) at Purdue University is home to many resources that you might find helpful at all stages of the writing process, including info and advice about getting started, overcoming writer's block, grammar and mechanics, and citation. It's easy to use, reliable, and free, so take advantage of it if you have a question not answered in this handbook.

How Can You Stay Involved with Writing at UCF?

Your first-year composition course represents only the first step in a larger writing experience at the university. Below, we've outlined some of the ways you might stay involved with writing after your composition course has ended.

Stylus: A Journal of First-Year Writing

http://writingandrhetoric.cah.ucf.edu/stylus/

The UCF Department of Writing and Rhetoric's First-Year Composition Program publishes *Stylus: A Journal of First-Year Writing* to provide a forum for the exemplary writing and research produced by students enrolled in Composition I and II at the university. Bringing together work from across a program of some four thousand students, *Stylus* celebrates writing that demonstrates an inquiring mind, compelling prose, and original thought.

Published online biannually in the fall and spring, the journal accepts work produced in composition classes by all students who are currently enrolled in the first-year writing program or who were enrolled the previous semester. All submissions go through an intensive peer review and selection process. Submission guidelines and procedure can be found on the *Stylus* Web site. Additionally, students interested in gaining editorial experience after completing their composition courses should contact the journal's editor for details.

President John C. Hitt Prize for Excellence in First-Year Writing

http://writingandrhetoric.cah.ucf.edu/stylus/hittprize.php

If *Stylus* represents the best of UCF's First-Year Composition Program, the President John C. Hitt Prize for Excellence in First-Year Writing is for the best of the best. Awarded yearly, the Hitt Prize recognizes the talent and hard work of one student published in either of the preceding fall or spring issues. This $500 award includes a $250 book scholarship provided by the President. More than the money, however, the Hitt Prize is a prestigious honor recognized by UCF faculty and administration as well as the larger academic community.

The Hitt Prize is named for UCF President John C. Hitt, whose commitment to undergraduate success has included using tuition differential money to lower class size in composition courses, hire additional full-time faculty to teach composition, and fully fund the University Writing Center.

Knights Write Showcase

http://writingandrhetoric.cah.ucf.edu/showcase.php

The Knights Write Showcase is an annual event held in the Pegasus Ballroom that provides a chance for students and faculty from across campus to get a glimpse of the exciting work currently going on in UCF's first-year composition classes. Activities include student displays, student and faculty panels, and the *Stylus* Awards Ceremony. The Hitt Prize is awarded at the Showcase, and awards are also given for best student displays.

To learn about previous Showcases and watch presentations by student panelists, visit the Knights Write Showcase website. Check with your professor for details on when the next Knights Write Showcase will be held and how to submit work for consideration.

UCF Undergraduate Research Journal

http://urj.ucf.edu

The mission of the *UCF Undergraduate Research Journal* (*URJ*) is to showcase articles of exemplary works from a wide range of student scholarship in all fields. The journal seeks outstanding research submitted by undergraduate students who have been involved in faculty-mentored research projects and activities related to scholarship. Issues are published online, so check out their previous issues to get a sense of the broad scope of research opportunities at UCF. Students interested in pursuing some of these opportunities should visit the Office of Undergraduate Research website at https://www.our.ucf.edu.

Become a University Writing Center Peer Tutor

http://uwc.cah.ucf.edu/become-a-consultant/

To assist writers across the disciplines, the University Writing Center (UWC) hires undergraduate and graduate tutors from a wide variety of majors. Tutors provide individual and small-group writing support to students, faculty, and staff from first-year to graduate in every discipline, while studying writing center research and theory. As they teach and learn in collaboration with others, tutors develop their own writing abilities, interpersonal skills, and leadership potential. Visit the UWC website to learn more about how to become a writing consultant.

Department of Writing and Rhetoric Undergraduate Programs

http://writingandrhetoric.cah.ucf.edu/

The UCF Department of Writing and Rhetoric offers three programs for undergraduate students: a B.A. in Writing and Rhetoric, a minor in Writing and Rhetoric, and an undergraduate certificate in professional writing. Students in these programs improve their writing and rhetorical knowledge and competencies, preparing them to be successful communicators in disciplinary, professional, and public contexts. Students undertake rigorous intellectual work to increase their effectiveness as writers, develop their facility with language, and deepen their engagement with writing as a form of social action. More information about these programs can be found on the Department of Writing and Rhetoric website.

B.A. in Writing and Rhetoric

The Bachelor of Arts degree in Writing and Rhetoric provides students with in-depth training in writing, rhetorical, and literacy studies, preparing them for a range of writing-focused jobs that involve the analysis, creation, editing, and coordination of texts, including digital and multimedia ones. In addition to preparing students for graduate/professional study and jobs across a variety of sectors (e.g. publishing and media, education, healthcare, marketing and public relations, entertainment and hospitality, civic organizations), the major prepares students to be more effective and ethical citizen-communicators.

Minor in Writing and Rhetoric

The Minor in Writing and Rhetoric is best suited for students planning to enter writing-intensive professions such as law, publishing and editing, journalism, public relations, marketing, communications management, and new media development. The minor prepares students to rhetorically analyze, effectively participate in, and critically reflect about writing experiences in their disciplines, professional workplaces, and community and civic environments. Students in the minor gain and apply historical and theoretical knowledge about rhetoric and writing. They also develop rhetorical and writing-related competencies and habits of mind that support effective and ethical communication in the twenty-first century. The minor is only 18 credit hours, which makes it convenient to add to a variety of majors.

Certificate in Public and Professional Writing

The 12-hour Certificate in Public and Professional Writing is appropriate for students in any major, including technical ones, as it can enhance their credentials for employment. The certificate provides students with additional training and experience in disciplinary, workplace, and public (e.g. civic, community-based) writing, preparing them to be effective, flexible professional communicators.

CHAPTER 2

Researching Writing and Literacy

Edited by Jacob Stewart

Over the course of your school experience, you have likely established some familiarity with the term "research." It's also likely that you have written a research paper, perhaps first encountering the assignment as early as middle school. You know how the assignment goes, right? Your instructor assigns or lets you pick a topic; you pull open your laptop or trudge down to the library; you read a few ideas from books or websites that discuss the subject; finally, you compile the knowledge you've located in a long document that includes appropriate citations.

This assignment with which you might be familiar includes what scholars refer to as ***topic-driven research***—you set out with to discover as much information as you can about a given subject and summarize it. This is an important skill set to have, and it is one that plays an important role in writing at the university level. It can help you gain a general understanding of knowledge in a field, help you understand what some important researchers have found, and help to stimulate your interest in a subject. Knowing the positive outcomes, middle and high school instructors begin to teach students to obtain topic-driven research skills from an early age.

However, at UCF and other American universities, this topic-driven approach to research is generally *not* the one used by scholars. Scholars rarely wake up in the morning and say to themselves "I think I'll research molecular biology today" or "perhaps I can investigate the history of U.S. agriculture." Research at the university level is not topic-driven but ***inquiry-driven***. Scholars observe the world around them and ask complex questions about what they see. Then, they conduct both primary and secondary research to help them seek answers to those questions.

As burgeoning scholars, this chapter will help you understand your research as motivated by inquiry. The chapter will assist you in understanding how to come to useful questions about your daily experiences, define the difference between primary and secondary research, lay out some useful primary research methods that you might employ in your freshman composition courses, and help you utilize the UCF library to find important past research that can contribute to answering your complex questions. Furthermore, the examples and discussion will be framed in such a way as to help you conduct research in the field of writing and literacy studies, specifically preparing you for success in your composition classes at UCF.

Through Research Writing, Enter The Conversation

In *On Rhetoric*, Aristotle argues "rhetoric may be defined as the faculty of observing in any given case the available means of persuasion." When you conduct research, you do so in order to answer your own research questions. But the research essay you compose after finding useful answers to those questions should be motivated by your desire to persuade an audience. You set out to persuade your readers that your answers are valid, useful, and contributive to a community's knowledge of the subject. Armed with your research data, you should intend to make a convincing argument. In thinking through this persuasive task, it might help you to use the metaphor of entering a conversation.

Throughout ancient times, dialogue appears alongside rhetoric. It was through dialogue that rhetoricians such as Aristotle, Isocrates, and Cicero taught their students rhetorical skills. Today, in the writing classroom, group discussion or pair dialogue is also part of the teaching process. A rhetorical text, too, is a conversation with previous texts, responding to ideas they have presented. In addition, arguments include paraphrases and quotes from others' compositions, making them part of the conversation. Moreover, writers composing texts must anticipate their audiences' reactions—questions they might ask or objections they might raise—so responses to these questions and objects can be included in the argument. This process of responding to audiences in advance continues the conversation.

So here you are, a new student with little experience in inquiry-based research and an instructor asking you to join academic conversations that are already in progress. How do you do that? How do you know what kind of response is appropriate? Have you ever entered a party where everyone is talking excitedly? Most likely, you paused near the doorway to get a sense of who was there and what they were discussing before you decided who to talk to and what to say. Or, have you become part of a Facebook group or a listserv discussion group? If so, you know it is a good idea to "lurk" for a while before asking questions or contributing a remark. Writing an academic paper involves a similar process. You read about a subject until you have a good grasp of the points authorities are debating. Then you find a way to integrate your own ideas and research results about that subject with the ideas of others and create an informed contribution to the conversation.

As a scholar who has performed thorough research to answer you complex questions, you gain an ability to be a key player in such scholarly conversations. In order to enter the conversation and to be a persuasive contributor, you will need lean on your research such that it supports your argument. The next section will introduce you two different categories of argument.

Navigating Aristotle's Artistic and Inartistic Proofs

Aristotle divided the process of writing and delivering a composition into five parts—invention, arrangement, style, memory, and delivery. The first of these was *invention*, during which the writer or speaker expanded a topic into ideas that were later arranged into a text or speech. According to the ancient Greeks, the rhetor *invented* these ideas, though they may have mirrored or adapted thoughts presented by previous rhetors. Today, we call this the **prewriting stage** of the writing process, an adaptation of Aristotle's invention stage.

The invention stage is an important aspect of writing that can help us distinguish between Aristotle's two types of proofs that are used when making a compelling argument—artistic and inartistic proofs.

Artistic Proofs

Artistic proofs are logical arguments constructed by rhetors from ideas plucked from their minds. An individual then develops these thoughts into a line of reasoning and, in the process, explores and narrows the topic, creates a thesis, and determines the ideas that need to be conveyed to the audience. These proofs are the ones that Aristotle and other ancient rhetoricians believed were critically important, for they are the ones developed from the *rhetor's own mind* and, thus, *invented*. Analytical research essays that you deliver to your professors or to other scholars in your academic field are full of artistic proofs. You make claims and draw conclusions about the subject of discussion and make rhetorical moves to persuade your readers of your position.

Inartistic Proofs

Within your research essay, you may also have several references to collected data or past events that are vital to making a compelling argument. We call these inartistic proofs. *Inartistic proofs* are direct evidence that the speaker might use to support the argument, such as testimony, documents, and anything else that rhetors do not invent through their own thinking. Today, we would call these proofs research. They, also, are essential to writing, but they should *support* the writer's ideas, rather than lead them.

Understanding the distinction between these proofs will go a long way in helping you to enter an academic conversation. The rest of this chapter will help you enter academic conversations by asking complex research questions and gather primary and secondary research data that will help you support your argument with inartistic proofs.

Doing Research Every Day

Although the words "research essay" sound imposing, to many students, research is really a natural part of your experience. You do research every day, often without being aware of the process, whether it is determining the calorie count of a serving of sugar-free ice cream or calculating the dollar amount you will spend on gasoline for a weekend trip. The information gathering you do for a research paper builds on the informal research skills you already have by adding additional places you look to for information and additional tools to use in that search. By going to the library or electronic databases to look for supportive authors, interviewing those who can provide important insight, conducting surveys, and observing groups of people, you expand your ability to write a persuasive research essay that helps you join the academic conversation.

In composition classes at UCF, you will be introduced to writing within a specific academic field—writing studies. One of the foundational principles of The Department of Writing and Rhetoric is that students are most successful when they have a focus area of research that helps to direct and contextualize their writing for class. But just because you are directed toward research about people's reading and writing development and practice doesn't mean your daily experiences and personal interests should be avoided. In fact, because you lead a complex writing life (whether you realize it or not) and because writing is such a prevalent part of your day-to-day interactions with others, you should embrace your own experiences when asking research questions about writing and literacy.

Think that it's a bit a stretch to say your everyday interests will be valuable to explore in the field of writing studies? Consider some of these successful projects conducted and completed by students in UCF composition courses (each of which is published in *Stylus: A Journal of First-Year Writing*).

What Do Students Write?

> **Cody Riebel** composed "Music and Literary Composition: The Revision Relation" in Professor Dan Martin's Composition II class. His research explores how songwriters revise during their composing process.
>
> **Allison Walter** composed "Where's the Beef: Communicating Vegetarianism in Mainstream America" in Professor Mary Tripp's Composition II class. Her research explores how vegetarians characterize their lifestyle choices through language choice in interactions with others who lead a more mainstream, meat-heavy, American lifestyle.
>
> **James Plyler** composed "Video Games and the Hero's Journey" in Professor Joseph Longhany's Composition II class. His research interrogates how narrative trends in video games reflect the archetype of the Hero's Journey, concluding they are a valid narrative medium.
>
> **Madeline Halvey** composed "Simple Forms of Dance and Movement Literacy" in Professor Kevin Roozen's Composition II class. She treats dance movement as a literate activity and questions its complex relationship with corresponding, written choreography.
>
> **Daniel Truesdell** composed "Constructing Identity in Academic Writing: A Case Study on Rhetorical Awareness in Engineering Discourse" in Professor Megan Lambert's Composition II class. His research seeks to find how engineering graduate students use rhetorical moves to construct their writing identity and how they perceive of rhetoric in helping them establish that identity.
>
> **Michael Nguyen** composed "Hang 'Em High and Bury 'Em Deep: Thematic Connections between Western and Zombie Fiction" in Professor Melissa Ringfield's Composition II class. He explores how the thematic lens of the Western genre can help readers better understand the genre convention of the Zombie film.

In this list, you can see that it was students' curiosity about their personal experiences that helped them conduct successful research and produce essays that were contributive to academic conversations. Each of these essays is clearly inquiry-based, as observation led the scholars to ask questions about the world around them.

Now that you've embraced the idea that your own experiences will be valuable in writing a successful, contributive research essay, how do you turn your daily observations into useful research questions? The answer to this question will be the focus of the next section.

Asking Useful Research Questions

Your research questions are the direct statements of your purpose in pursuing a research subject. They clearly outline what you hope to learn by the end of your research endeavor. Research questions are not unique to composition courses or writing and literacy studies. Progress in all academic fields occurs because scholars ask useful questions and provide potential answers to those questions (which generally leads other scholars to ask further questions, as is the nature of any engaging conversation). Whether you're an aspiring engineer, literary scholar, chemist, psychologist, or have any other career goal, asking useful research questions will help you become a contributive scholar in your field.

How do you begin formulating useful research questions? As we have stated previously in this chapter, useful research begins with your daily observations. You observe the world around you, and ask questions. People conduct research in order to answer these questions. They seek answers by reading informed commentators and scholars (*secondary research*) or perform field research by asking questions of informed people, creating experiments, observing how people interact, or reading texts critically (*primary research*). People do research because they are unwilling to let their questions go unanswered.

Here are some useful tips that can help you formulate useful research questions:

Avoid binary questions:

- Generally, if the answer to your question can be either "yes" or "no," then you haven't yet arrived at a useful research question. "Yes" or "no" responses generally leave other academics little room for response. Therefore, those questions carry little potential for carrying an academic conversation forward.

Embrace complexity:

- If your research question seems to have an obvious answer or is one to which you already know the answer, it's best to ask another question. Obvious answers won't interest scholars. And a question to which you already know the answer won't help you learn anything.

Ask questions about "how" things might work, "why" things work as they do, or "what" the consequences are of some policy. Some examples might include:

- How can UCF promote increased campus security measures while still maintaining the image that campus security isn't a problem?

- Why does UCF require a C- or higher in composition classes in order for a student to pass? What are the consequences of this policy?

- What are the consequences of allowing multiple groups to occupy the UCF free speech space simultaneously during the first week of classes?

Preliminary questions about your daily observations are often far too broad to actually be answered by research. Broad questions often lead to broad answers that don't contribute to academic conversations. After arriving at your initial inquiries, you need to take time to refine your questions. You can do this by contextualizing your research and responding to the current academic conversation.

Narrowing Questions through Contextualization

Consider that you want to write a paper about social media. You might spend a few hours a day engaging various social media platforms such as Facebook, Twitter, and Instagram. You connect with your friends and family on those platforms, get your news from them, and do daily research using them. This certainly seems like a fruitful topic to be studying. In trying to formulate a research question, you state "How do social media platforms help people communicate?" But this question is far too broad. There are too many social media platforms and too many types of communication for this question to ever really be answered. Therefore, you need to narrow your focus. In order to narrow your question, try to think of communication on social media in a particular context. Context means the specific environment in which a text, phenomena, discussion, or experience occurs. Elements in the context can include place, time, events, and people.

Sometimes it can be difficult to narrow the question because you are over-whelmed by its initial breadth. First, you might try making a list of your daily interactions on social media. This can be a useful activity no matter what questions you are interested in. Making a list of your daily observations can help you understand the various, specific research questions you might pursue. Figure 2-1 shows a list of potential daily observations about social media. It outlines a few platforms, communication activities, and groups that might occur daily for someone like you on social media.

Platforms used daily	Groups and uses
· Facebook · Twitter · Reddit · Snapchat · Instagram · Medium · LinkedIn · YouTube	· See what my family is doing · Check out sports news · Seek political opinions · Check to see if my marching band director changed practice time · Watch funny commercials · Post about video games · Take a picture of my lunch and post · Share cool or important stories

Figure 2-1

Once you have your list, select a specific avenue to pursue. Your initial question "How do social media platforms help people communicate?" might be reformed as "How does Twitter function in communication between a presidential candidate and potential voters?" Or "What impact does language use on Facebook have on the way a high school band operates?" Both of these questions have been pursued by students in UCF composition courses. They are specific and contextualized in the sense that they investigate particular interactions on particular social media platforms.

TIP

Sometimes, contextualization also has to do with your specific environment as a writer and researcher. You might be interested in seeing how language use differs during practices of NBA and college basketball teams. This has potential to lead to some cool research questions and a great essay. But, as a student at UCF, do you have access to a professional team's practice? Are you going to be able to interview players and ask them about why they made certain decisions with language? Probably not. Asking useful research questions also has to take into account what questions you will actually be able to answer based on who you are as a researcher and what information you have access to.

Narrowing Questions by Entering an Academic Conversation

In some cases, you can narrow your too broad research questions by reading what other authors have said about a topic. In an academic conversation, authors are often interacting to answer some of those broad questions, each offering insight into a particular piece of a very complex puzzle. By reading what other authors have said about a topic, you can start to see what those authors *haven't* researched. This provides you the opportunity ask specific questions that haven't been answered. The benefit of this approach is that you know the answer to your research question will be contributive to the academic conversation before you begin.

In some cases, you will develop a specific research question and then begin to read what other authors have said about your research subject, only to find that your question has already been answered. Don't panic! This means you are entering into an academic pursuit that is clearly worthwhile. Instead of getting frustrated, read what that author has to say about the issue, and then slightly alter your question to ask something related but not fully covered in the author's work. You might also consider asking a question that the researcher did not have time to cover, responding to their calls for further research (often found in the conclusion of scholarly articles), testing their ideas in a different context, or using different methods to discover new perspectives on the question.

Questions about Writing and Literacy in Composition at UCF

Research questions in composition courses at UCF, with a few exceptions, are generally concerned with contextualized instances of writing and literacy. You learn to navigate genres used by particular communities, research how language causes members of communities to interact, and begin to understand how writing (in a broad sense that includes more than just text inscription) has shaped your own experience of the world around you. When beginning to ask research questions about writing and literacy, observations of your own writing practices and experiences can help you find your research foundation.

Remember our earlier list of successful student research essays from UCF composition courses? These research questions were either directly stated in their essays or are close approximations of the questions they answered with their research:

Cody Riebel, "Music and Literary Composition: The Revision Relation"
- "What is the relationship between the revising processes of musicians and writers?"

Allison Walter, "Where's the Beef: Communicating Vegetarianism in Mainstream America"
- "How do vegetarians and non-vegetarians negotiate their differences through their communication styles and behavioral choices, and why?"
- "What factors—inside and out—play a role in how these conversations are approached or handled?"

James Plyler, "Video Games and the Hero's Journey"
- What characteristics of video game narratives demonstrate that they represent a legitimate narrative form and why?
- How can the theory of monomyth be used to characterize the narratives of video games?

Madeline Halvey, "Simple Forms of Dance and Movement Literacy"
- "Do literate forms of dance have to be fully comprehensive in order to serve a purpose in the dance realm?"
- "Can simpler forms of movement literacy be those that are most beneficial for dance pedagogy?"

Daniel Truesdell, "Constructing Identity in Academic Writing: A Case Study on Rhetorical Awareness in Engineering Discourse"
- How do engineering students construct their identity through rhetorical choices in written discourse? Do their perceived identities correlate with these written identities? Why or why not?

Michael Nguyen, "Hang 'Em High and Bury 'Em Deep: Thematic Connections between Western and Zombie Fiction"
- What value can be found in using the Western genre as an alternative analytical framework for understanding zombie fiction?

Once you've established a useful research question it's time to start considering how to answer it. The remainder of this chapter will explore primary and secondary research methods that will help you in conducting successful, academic research.

Primary and Secondary Research Methods

If you've bought a set of headphones lately, chances are you did some research when you decided which brand you would buy. To begin with, you already had some knowledge of headphones and brand names. Maybe you heard someplace that the balance was good with one brand or that another brand's product got damaged too easily. You listened to friends' headphones and you knew which brands are popular and which produce clear sound. You didn't have to look in a book for that information. It is just part of your everyday knowledge. You may not use it everyday, but it's there when you need it.

Once you explored your knowledge of headphones by thinking about what you already knew, you probably visited an electronics store and listened to several sets. Maybe you asked the salesperson about the model you were interested in, and asked friends about their headphones and how much they liked them. You might have consulted a buying guide that rates headphones and gave you suggestions on the sound quality, reliability, and value of several different headphones. You might also have looked at a few reviews of equipment in magazines at a local bookstore. If you did any or all of these things, then you are already familiar with basic primary and secondary research.

Primary research involves personal interaction with your subject. Interviews from people on the scene of an event, questionnaires, and observation are all primary sources. Novels, poems, diaries, and fictional films are also primary sources because they stand alone and are not interpreting anything else.

Secondary research involves the reading and gathering of ideas that interpret the subject for you. This includes magazine articles, books, websites discussing your research, and scholarly peer-reviewed articles (perhaps the most important for your current academic setting). The library research you've done for your previous middle school and high school classes is most likely secondary research.

Most writing assignment in composition classes at UCF ask you to combine your own experience or primary research with information gained from secondary research in books or periodicals. For example, you might be asked to write an essay about recycling. You can include your own experience with recycling or visit a recycling center in your community and report what you see. You can also support this primary research with secondary research in books or periodicals in which authorities offer facts and opinions about the effectiveness of recycling. In addition, you can interview an authority on recycling, perhaps a professor or chairperson of a community committee.

Now that you have established a distinction between primary and secondary research methods, the next section will discuss several potential methods of primary research that you can engage in both within your UCF composition classes and in some future academic and professional settings.

Primary Research Methods

Your research should be inquiry-driven. Therefore, you the primary research you conduct should be responsive to your questions. Making a decision about what type of primary research data to gather should not be an arbitrary choice. Think about the questions you are trying to answer, and select the research methods that are best suited to answering those questions. Do you want to see an in-depth profile of a particular type of writer's process? **Case study**, which will be discussed below, seems like an appropriate research method. But taking a **survey** of many people seems less appropriate to the task. Selecting the right research methods means having a clear understanding of what answers you seek. The following sections lay out some possible primary research methods that you might use when researching writing, literacy, or several other areas of study.

Ethnograpy

The root "ethno" means "people" or "culture." Combined with "graphy," which means a "description or image," ethnography can be thought of as a description of a group of people or culture in context. Ethnography is founded on the idea the best way to get a full understanding of how people interact is to actually observe groups of people in their environment. This should be done without being intrusive, and often ethnography is carried out when the researcher is a member of the group being studied (we call this participant observation). In writing studies, we use ethnography as a way of understanding how writing functions in a community and how communication serves to trigger interactions between people. A researcher may have some hypotheses about what they will find while observing the group, but generally the observation will dictate the results of the study. You might not have a clear idea of what you will find in observation. But you will leave the observation with a great deal more knowledge than you had previously. Ethnography can help writing studies scholars:

- Identify how texts and text genres operate in the environment
- Identify how individuals communicate around texts in the environment
- Identify how individuals gain, maintain, and assert authority through communication in the environment
- Identify how any other element in the situation impacts writing or literacy

In his excellent Composition II research essay, "The Game within the Games: The Behaviors, Language, and Virtual Norms of *RuneScape*," Matthew Ceriale uses an ethnographic approach to interrogate how the jargon of online game players is attached to social norms and behaviors in the *Runescape* environment. By combining a thorough analysis of the genres of the *Runescape* community, observation of community members playing the game, and interviews with community members, Ceriale was able to trace patterns in language that indicated particular types of community behaviors. His full study can be read in the Spring 2013 issue of *Stylus*.

Case Study

Case studies share similar characteristics with ethnography in that both methods are interested in ascertaining a clear picture of peoples' writing in context. But while ethnography seeks to obtain a picture of a whole writing community or environment, case study attempts to understand a specific activity or the actions of an individual. In writing studies, we use case studies in order to gain thorough insight into how, why, and when an individual writes or performs some particular activity. Case studies involve observing an individual in context and describing what is observed. A key element of successful case studies is the use of extensive interviews that seek out in-depth understanding of the participants writing history and activity. Case studies can help writing studies scholars understand:

- How an individual's environment or community leads them to write and communicate
- How an individual's writing history contributes to their writing behaviors or identity

Camilla Perez successfully uses the case study method with three participants in her "Spanglish" and Its Effects on L1 and L2." The well-planned case studies looked closely at the participants' history of language and writing by conducting hour-long interviews, observations, and analyzing their response to a writing prompt. She was able to use the resulting data to argue that "Spanglish" is a third language that develops as students attempt to assimilate English as a second language. Her full study can be read in the Spring 2013 Knights Write Showcase Special issue of *Stylus*.

Survey

Surveys are used in a variety of fields in order to get a clear understanding of trends in large populations. Surveys are commonly used in writing studies when attempting to gain insight into the writing habits of many writers in an environment. If attempting to draw some conclusions about all first year writing students at UCF, it might make more sense to survey a representative sample of those students, if access to all of them is unavailable. These smaller survey portions allow you to trace some tentative trends and lead toward useful questions that you or other researcher can answer. When composing a survey, it's important to identify the exact population you want to participate and make any assumptions made in the survey clear in the written results. Writing studies scholars use surveys to:

- Understand the perspectives of multiple writers
- Explore the impact of a particular writing environment, prompt, class, etc. on several writers
- Trace trends in writing perspectives that can lead to questions requiring more in-depth analysis

In "Preparing to Be a Doctor in High School: A Study of Underrepresented Pre-Medical Students' Gains from Advanced Placement (AP) Courses," Sara Bolivar Wagers deployed a survey to several UCF students majoring in science fields. By limiting her focus to science-related majors and identifying success rates of underrepresented student populations in AP course, Wagers was able to conduct a follow-up focus group that helped answer more complex questions. She was able to conclude that success in AP Chemistry and Biology was not the only predetermining factor in success as a UCF science major. Her entire study can be read in the Spring 2014 Knights Write Showcase Special Issue of *Stylus*.

Archival Research (*contributions made to this section by Professor Marcy Galbreath*)
Archival research engages in the use of library physical or digital archives in order to develop a historical perspective on a research subject that can inform our understanding of present developments. In writing studies, archival research is often used to understand trends in writing and course history; it is also often used as a means of tracing histories through written-documents by performing textual analysis on them as "rhetorical artifacts." News clippings, photographs, pamphlets, memos, and messages are just a few of the many rhetorical artifacts that can be analyzed when performing archival research. Writing studies scholars use archival research in order to:

- Trace the historical development of writing procedures in a particular context or environment and understand this history's influence on the present
- Trace the development of a location, population, or culture's history through textual analysis of historical documents referred to as rhetorical artifacts.

In his Composition II study "A Historical Approach to the Progression of LGBTQ Treatment and Acceptance at the University of Central Florida," Jacob Smith uses the John C Hitt collection in the UCF library archives to gain a historical perspective on UCF's acceptance of Lesbian, Gay, Bisexual, Transsexual, and Questioning community on campus. Through analysis of several historical documents, including a Newcomer Packet distributed to members of the Gay, Lesbian, and Bisexual Student Union from 1994, Smith concludes that the UCF community was ahead of national trends in acceptance of the LGBTQ community. His full study can be read in Spring 2014 issue of *Stylus*.

Textual Analysis
Textual analysis is the breaking down of a particular text in order to ascertain its underlying themes, motivations, purposes, and rhetorical impact. Specifically, textual analysis interrogates specific passages or portions of texts in order to determine their meaning in an identified context. Textual analysis is at the heart of writing studies scholarship, and many of the other methods in this section require some use of textual analysis. Some of us become familiar with textual analysis in high school by performing literary analysis in which we try to draw conclusions about the themes of a novel. Textual analysis in writing studies does not necessarily require the object of study be literature (poetry, novels, short stories, etc.) though it certainly can interrogate such genres. Textual analysis tries to understand a subject text as it is situated in a cultural, environmental, or community context. The types of texts that can be analyzed are limitless (and can include non-print objects), but the aim is to try to understand how and why a text came to exist in the way that it did. These are just a few of the phenomena that writing scholars use textual analysis in order to understand:

- The ideological motivations of a text
- The impact of a text on a given audience
- The narrative themes of a text and their impact
- The power relationships between author of the text and its readers
- How a text in contextualized within a community or context
- How a text helps to shape community and group communication standards
- How a text initiates particular types of conversations

In her ENC1102 study "Exploiting the American Dream: The Political Rhetoric of Julian Castro," Katelyn Van De Water textually analyzes San Antonio Mayor Julian Castro's speech at the 2012 Democratic Nation Convention. Van De Water pulls particular passages from Castro's speech that show him drawing on the theme of "The American Dream" shared by the audience in order to promote the presidential candidacy of Barak Obama and discredit the candidacy of Mitt Romney. Her full study can be read in the Fall 2013 issue of *Stylus*.

In the following sections, three types of textual analysis often used by writing and literacy scholars are summarized in detail: **rhetorical analysis, genre analysis, and multimodal text analysis**.

Rhetorical Analysis

Writing and literacy scholars often seek to discover why a particular argument was structured or delivered in a specific way. Rhetorical analysis allows researchers in many disciplines to find the motivations for and impact of a piece of discourse on its audience. When using the method, researchers look closely at both the text and the real-world environment in which the text was written (within what time, place, institution, etc.). These observations help the researcher understand how the purpose, writer/speaker (sometimes referred to as the rhetor), audience, and environment influenced the construction of the argument and its intended or unintended effects. We often call this placing a text in its *rhetorical situation*. Writing and rhetoric scholars use rhetorical analysis to:

- Discover the motivations of the writer/speaker
- Understand why the writer/speaker made particular language choices
- Determine how the environment surrounding the text assisted or inhibited the writer/speaker from achieving their intended goals
- Interrogate how the writer/speaker and audience negotiate what is considered effective language in the environment
- Understand how audiences are likely to react to a particular argument

In his Composition I essay, "Intertextuality and Understanding Dave Chappelle's Comedy," David Galvez uses effective rhetorical analysis to interrogate the reason that a particular skit performed by the comedian was effective as a comic text. Galvez argues that Chappelle's comedic depiction of President George W. Bush at the U.N. was effective because it took into account his audience's perspectives—their disagreement with Bush's policies and their affiliation with African American culture.

Galvez argues that this clear understanding of audience rendered Chappelle's comic text effective. His full study can be read in the Spring 2011 issue of *Stylus*.

Genre Analysis

In the context of writing studies, genres are texts that are distinguished by their repeated and predictable characteristics and that arise in separate but similar rhetorical situations. Genre analysis tends to give additional attention to formatting and structural features that is not always present in rhetorical analysis. If you were to picture a syllabus in your head and describe what it looks like and what kind of information it contains, what would you point out? You would probably say that syllabi tend to include the name of the course, contact information for the professor, or a grading scale. Over and over again, instructors need to prepare students for the class by offering them contact information, a course description, a course calendar, etc. "The syllabus" is a textual genre with repeated and predictable characteristics. You know what's coming even before you receive it. Furthermore, genres lead to real-world actions and cause conversations between community members that have important effects on the community's environment. You can probably list several actions you take after reading a syllabus, for example. When writing scholars perform genre analysis, they look for repeated features across examples of a genre and attempt to figure out the motivation and function of continuing to use them in similar (or varying) ways. Looking closely at genres can help us see how communities deploy discourse and communication in accordance with their goals, values, and beliefs. Writing and rhetoric scholars use genre analysis to:

- Understand the complex ways in which communities use texts to communicate among members
- Understand how communities use texts to recruit new members
- Understand how communities use language to represent their values to community members and non-community members
- Understand how communities characterize the world around them and why
- Understand how communities achieve their goals

In her Composition II study, "The Genres of Chi Omega: An Activity Analysis," Victoria Marro analyzed the genres employed by Chi Omega including its national magazine, chapter newsletter, announcements, chapter websites, and rule books. Combined with **text-based interviews**, Marro was able to place each of these genres into the varying contexts of different chapters of Chi Omega. She found that each specific chapter used different genres based on what functioned the best in their particular context. However, each chapter used their genres to mediate goals shared across all chapters of the Chi Omega community. Her full study can be read in the Spring 2012 issue of *Stylus*.

Multimodal Text Analysis (contributions to this section by Professor Yumani Davis)

As digital technologies have developed, it has become increasingly necessary for writing scholars to recognize the multimodal nature of texts when considering how they function within communities and contexts. Multimodal text analysis is the process of textual analysis that questions how textual, visual, auditory, and other text elements operate to deliver messages and meaning. In the below screenshot, you can see how one might interrogate a website, for example (developed by Professor Yumani Davis):

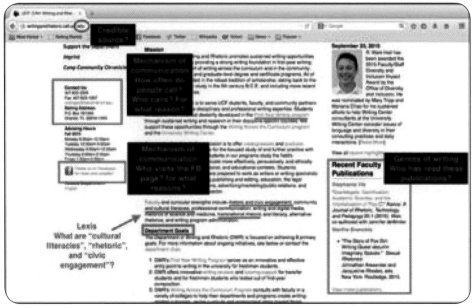

Figure 2-2: Screenshot

In this example, we can see how questions are being asked of the textual features of a digital publication, the Department of Writing and Rhetoric website. Skills in reading multimodal genres are also used in analysis, such as where the credibility of the page is tested by its URL. Multimodal text analysis allows writing and rhetoric scholars to:

- Understand the relationship between visual, textual, auditory, etc. features of a text and how those features mediate the message of the author
- Understand how audiences of the multimodal text are likely to react to its features
- Understand how various mechanisms of communication are deployed in context
- Understand how rhetors use digital technologies to effectively or ineffectively persuade audiences

In her Composition II study, "Looking Through the Semiotic Lens: Rhetorical Sponsors of Civic Engagement in Cyberpublics," Paige Preston analyzes three blogs of varying content, *Humans of New York, Dress Profesh,* and *Blue Velvet: Re-dressing New Orleans in Katrina's Wake* in order to understand their use of rhetoric to promote civic engagement by their readers. She successfully interrogates the textual and visual elements of the blogs in order to determine that the blogs promote civic awareness and engagement in online spaces also known as cyberpublics. According to Preston, each blog uses rhetoric to undermine "entrenched, social truths." Her full study can be read in the Fall 2015 issue of *Stylus*.

Interviews

Interviews are conducted in conjunction with several of the primary methods mentioned in this section. Therefore, below there are several tips that can help you conduct a useful interview.

Your community probably has some excellent sources sitting behind desks at the nearest college, city hall, or federal office building. You also probably have some useful contacts that can help you find answers to your inquiries. If you are looking into the environment, you could contact the Environmental Protection Agency, an attorney who specializes in environmental law, a professional employee of the park system or the Bureau of Land Management, a college professor who works in the natural sciences, or a group in your area dedicated to beautification and restoration efforts. If you don't know anyone connected with these organizations, a look in the yellow pages or blue government pages of the phone book should give you the information you need.

Once you've scheduled the interview, make a list of questions you ask your interview subject. There are two types of questions you can ask your subject: open and closed. *Open questions* such as the following leave room for extended discussion because they don't have a yes, no, or specific answer:

- Could you tell me about the most positive experience you've had with [topic]?
- When did you decide to study [topic]?
- What's the most negative experience you've had with [topic]?

Questions like these allow for extended discussions. Even if it seems your subject has finished his or her response to the question, let a few moments of silence pass before you ask another question. Silence can be uncomfortable for some people, and he or she might feel compelled to expand on the response to your question in interesting ways.

Closed questions are useful for gathering specific information. Questions such as "When did you graduate?" and "How long have you been involved in [topic]?" are closed questions. Although closed questions are important to an interview, be sure they're balanced by questions that allow your subject room to talk and expand on his or her ideas.

Although you've prepared a list of questions you'll want to follow, don't be afraid to ask a question that isn't on your list. If your subject mentions briefly an experience that seems relevant to your topic, you might want to ask him or her more about that experience, even though it isn't on your list of questions. Indeed, the best way to interview may be to read over your questions just before you meet your subject, then not refer to them during the interview. Before you leave, however, look over your list to see if you have missed any questions of importance. Remember to let lulls in the conversation work for you by drawing your interview subject into further explanations or illustrations of previous comments. If you interview a talkative person who strays from the topic, try to steer him or her back to the questions you've prepared, but if you can't, don't worry. You'll probably get useful information anyway. Be courteous and attentive. Even if you're recording the interview, take notes. It makes both the subject and the interviewer feel more comfortable and serves as a backup, should your recording not work.

For a useful example of how to effectively use interview in order to answer complex research questions, see Yadilex Ali's "The Shift in Parental Literacy Sponsorship and Its Value According to the Children of Immigrants." Ali uses interviews in her case study of three children of immigrant in order to understand how their various experiences led to different types of experiences with reading and writing. She interrogates her participants' responses in order to draw complex conclusions about the relationship between immigrant parents and their children as students. Her full study can be read in the Fall 2015 issue of *Stylus*.

Text-based Interviews (*contributions to this section by Professor Kevin Roozen*) – s are a useful subset of the interview method. As writing studies scholars, we try to discover the value, purposes, and composing history of a text situated in a context. Sometimes we are able to ascertain this through text analysis, ethnographic observation, or other methods. But it can also be very useful ask the author or users of a text questions about its uses, purposes, and development. You might ask your research participant(s) some of the following questions after reading the collected text (developed by Professor Kevin Roozen):

- What function or purpose does this text serve? What work does it do?
- Who created this text? Who uses this text, and what do they use it for?
- What can you tell me about how this text got created?
- What kinds of talk occur when people use this text?
- How long have you been using these kinds of texts?
- How did you learn to use this text and other texts like it?
- Where is this text kept?
- How many different people have likely seen this text?
- What kinds of technologies were used in the production and use of this text?
- Does this text get used in conjunction with other kinds of texts? If so, which ones?
- Does this text lead to other kinds of texts? If so, which ones?

In her *Stylus* published "Fanfiction, Poetry, Blogs, and Journals: A Case Study of the Connection between Extracurricular and Academic Writings," Marissa Penzato challenges some of the conclusions drawn by professional writing studies scholar Nancy Sommers regarding the inexperience of student writers. In order to show student writing processes to be more complicated than Penzato believes Sommers outlines, the author performs case studies with four fanfiction writers. Penzato reads several examples of her case study participants' fanfiction, blogs, and poetry. After developing questions based on her reading, she interviewed her participants based on the texts. By asking participants how their texts developed, Penzato links their writing experiences to their writing processes and identities. Her full study can be read in the Spring 2012 issue of *Stylus*.

Tracing Patterns in Primary Research Data
(*contributions to this section by Professor Lissa Pompos Mansfield*)

Now that you've successfully conducted your primary research with one of these methods, it's time to make sense of the resulting data. In qualitative research, we call things like interview responses, texts that you analyze, and observations of communities "data," even though they are not quantifiable. At the end of your research, the amount of data can be somewhat daunting. So how do you make sense of all of this? The following handout developed by UCF Professor Lissa Pompos Mansfield will help you get started.

Ways to Look for "Themes" or Recurring Ideas in Your Primary, Qualitative Data

An adapted list of nine steps

(Adapted from: Ryan, Gery W., and Bernard, H. Russell. "Techniques to Identify Themes in Qualitative Data." http://www.analytictech.com/mb870/readings/ryan-bernard_techniques_to_identify_themes_in.htm)

1. **Look for repeating words and phrases**. If a word or phrase shows up many times in your interview or observation data, take note of it. Count how many times it surfaces. The fact that this word or phrase is frequently used might suggest that it is important. These words might also summarize a key idea. Be sure to note synonyms of the word or phrase. If the repeated word is "power," for example, pay attention to words like "authority," too.

2. **Pay attention to "indigenous categories."** Indigenous words are "local terms that may sound unfamiliar or are used in unfamiliar ways." (They are similar to the specialized vocabulary of a particular group, or "lexis.") In addition to noting these unique words, pay attention to how they are used and how they are organized into the group's vocabulary. (Are there multiple versions of the same word? What versions of words are used most often?)

3. **Note Key Words in Context [KWICs].** Similar to the two steps listed above, be sure to note not only the key words a group uses, but also HOW they are used. According to Ryan and Russell, "if you want to understand a concept, then look at how it is used. In this technique, researchers identify key words and then systematically search the…text to find all instances of the word or phrase. Each time they find a word, they make a copy of it and its immediate context. Themes get identified by physically sorting the examples into piles of similar meaning."

4. **Compare and contrast texts**. Try "interviewing" (or asking questions about) your text by studying each line of your transcript or notes separately. Then, compare the previous line to the next line. Some questions to keep in mind while you study each line/note are: "What is this [line/sentence/note/statement] about?," "How does it differ from the preceding or following statements?," "What kinds of things [like ideas or key words] are mentioned in both?," and "What does [this statement] remind me of [based on other things I have read]?"

5. **Approach the data like a social scientist**. Pay attention to things like "evidence of social conflict, cultural contradictions, informal methods of social control, things that people do in managing impersonal social relationships, methods by which people acquire and maintain achieved and ascribed status, and information about how people solve problems." Also note the setting and context of your observations, the perspectives of the people you interview and observe, and their ways of thinking about "people, objects, processes, activities, events, and relationships."

6. **Search for missing information**. What is not mentioned in your data? Is something absent, and why might that be the case? Sometimes, the fact that

people DON'T discuss something hints at its importance. Also, absences in your data can point to assumptions the person/group makes. (For example, the president of an organization might not state the reasons for taking a specific action because he/she assumes that all other members of the group already know those reasons.)

7. **Decipher metaphors and analogies**. Look for examples of when the person/group describes a concept in terms of a metaphor, analogy, or simile; this is a common way for people to relate their thoughts, behaviors, or feelings about an experience to some other idea. If a metaphor is used, determine the meaning of the comparison. For example, if your interviewee says "our group works like a well-oiled machine," they are comparing the group to an object that has connotations of labor/work, power, and other ideas.

8. **Look at transitions between ideas**. In both written and oral communication, writers/ speakers take turns communicating and often mark their progression between ideas with words like "so," "now," "then," "next," "also," "in addition," "because," etc. According to Ryan and Russell, "In written texts, new paragraphs are often used by authors to indicate either subtle or abrupt shifts in topics. In oral speech, pauses, change in tone, or particular phrases may indicate thematic transitions." Paying attention to transitions might help you to see how talk is divided between participants, how ideas and topics change over time, etc.

9. **Look at connectors**. Pay attention to words or phrases that "indicate relationships among things." If there is a causal (cause and effect) relationship between ideas, words like "because," "since," and "as a result" might be used. If there is a conditional (if/then) relationship between ideas, words like "if," "then," "rather than," and "instead of" might be used. If there is a chronological relationship between ideas, words like "before," "after," "then," and "next" might be used.

Advice for Visualizing Your Themes:

❶ **Mark up your texts.** Use highlighters, underlining, and other "marking" tools to help you note important pieces of data or passages of text.

❷ **Scan (or "eyeball") texts to see what stands out.** Oftentimes, the most prominent words or features of a document also hint at the main ideas of a text.

❸ **Cut, sort, and reassemble.** When you know that certain pieces of data (such as a quote or a note) are important, but you don't know how these pieces fit into the "big picture" of your theme, cut them into separate pieces. Then, look at all your pieces separately and try to group them together based on similar ideas or features. When you have these groups, determine what each piece in the group has in common with the other pieces and why this commonality might be important. These large groups might give you some hints at the larger "theme."

Secondary Research and Instructor Expectations

You have been assigned a research paper or project. What does your professor expect of you when gathering secondary sources?

First, always remember that research is an iterative process. Conducting secondary research in the library will never be like waving a magic wand, where you plug in a search word and "POOF!" you find all of the sources that you need. Rather, secondary research is an exercise in critical thinking. You need to be able to consider what you are looking for and be prepared to try something different when you don't initially get the results that you want. The UCF library has a great many resources located in various catalogs and databases that you will need to navigate in order to find useful secondary resources and enter important academic conversations. Luckily, there are several people and texts, including this handbook, that can help you find useful sources for your project.

It's important that you understand the assignment: What specifically does your professor want you to research? Do you have instructions about what kinds of sources your professor wants? Are restrictions put on what Internet or database sources you can use? Possibly, your instructor has specified that you need to use books, journals, major magazines and newspapers, and certain web-based information. This means that you are to use reputable sources to obtain a balanced, impartial viewpoint about your topic. So, how do you find these sources?

- **Books**: In these days of easy-to-find resources on the Internet, students may wonder why to bother with books at all. However, scholarly books treat academic topics with in-depth discussion and careful documentation of evidence. College libraries collect scholarly books that are carefully researched and reviewed by authorities in the book's field. Look for recently published books rather than older books, even if they are on your topic. Academic books or well-researched popular books often have bibliographies or lists of additional references at the end of the book. These lists are useful for two reasons: first, if such lists of books are present, it is a good clue this is a well-researched book, and, second, it gives you a ready list of other possible resources you can consult for your research project.

- **Scholarly journals**: Just having the word "journal" in the title does not mean it is a journal. *Ladies Home Journal,* or the *Wall Street Journal,* for example, are not journals. Your instructor means peer-reviewed journals in which the authors have documented their sources. Peer-reviewed means that articles have been reviewed by experts in the field for reliability and relevance before being published. Your library should have print indexes to journals in which you can look up your topic. You may also be able to find journal articles—sometimes in full text—through the online databases offered by your college library.

- **Major magazines and newspapers:** These publications report the news based on actual observation of events and interviews with experts and also present informed editorial opinions. Examples are magazines, such as *Time, Newsweek,* and *U.S. News and World Report;* newspapers such as the *New York Times,* the *Boston Globe,* the *Wall Street Journal,* and the *Washington Post.* You can locate full-text articles directly from the online versions of major print magazines and newspapers. Often, these publications charge a fee for articles not published recently. However, you can often find the same articles free through one of your library databases.

TIP Be careful not to confuse these popular journals with the peer-reviewed journals mentioned previously. Learn to tell the difference between popular and scholarly articles/journals by using the UCF Library's online modules available at http://infolit.ucf.edu/

- **Special Interest Publications**: These are periodicals that focus on a specific topic but are written for a wider audience than are scholarly journals. Authors of articles base their articles on interviews with experts, recent scholarly books and journals, and other reputable sources. Examples include *Psychology Today* and *Scientific American.*

- **Government Documents:** Government documents present a wealth of information for many contemporary events and issues. Your library may be a federal depository, which means that users can locate many federal documents onsite. If so, you can look up government sources in the online library catalog. Government documents are also available though online databases. As seen above in the primary research methods section, these documents can sometimes be used as primary sources when conducting archival research.

- **Encyclopedias**: Encyclopedias can be useful to browse when you are looking for topics. They are also helpful for providing background information such as dates when events occurred. However, most instructors prefer that you do not use encyclopedias as sources you cite in your paper. This is particularly true for Wikipedia, the online encyclopedia that is assembled by volunteers who have specialized knowledge on topics and, thus, has no systematic vetting of the contents. However, Wikipedia entries often include bibliographies which can be useful in pointing you to books, articles, or other websites which can be used as references.

- **Internet**: The problem with web-based information is that anyone with some knowledge of computers can put up a website on the Internet. Thus, information from websites must be carefully evaluated as to author, publishing organization, etc. One way to deal with this problem is to find web information through the librarian-generated indexes and search engines which screen websites for credibility (See list later in this chapter).

As you use the categories above to find sources for your paper or project, realize that your topic influences your choice of reference materials. If you are writing about a literary topic such as Shakespeare's *Othello,* you will find a number of relevant books and journal articles. If your topic is more contemporary, such as the current status of the country's housing market, you may be able to find some books or journal articles for background information, but you will need to use recent magazine and newspaper articles to find the latest information.

As you examine your sources, remember that gathering the information should help you discover what you think about your topic, not just what others think. This will enable you to create a paper based on your ideas and opinions, with source materials supporting your position. And this will ultimately allow you to contribute to the ongoing, academic conversation.

Employ Computerized Library Catalogs

Public Access Catalogs (PACs) or computerized catalogs have replaced card catalogs. A library computerized catalog provides bibliographical information about the library's collection, including thousands of books, photos, videos, journals, and other items. Generally, catalogs can be accessed by keyword, subject, author, title, and call number. You may also find books which are available in digital form through the catalog. In addition, on the library home page, you will find links to other information and services such as database searches, interlibrary loan, and course reserves.

The UCF library provides access to its catalog through its homepage, library.ucf. edu. Navigating the library catalog requires the use of its central element, the search interface at the center of the site. As can be seen in the screenshot, students can search for articles, books, and videos, as well as perform a quick search of the library catalogs. It isn't always the easiest task to navigate the library catalog; the homepage also provide access to the "Ask Us" feature, giving you the option to call, email, or chat with a librarian. Don't be afraid to make use of this function. Research librarians can be very valuable friends when trying to locate secondary sources.

Figure 2-3: UCF Libraries Screenshot

When searching the library catalog, you have several options for attempting to locate sources through the central search feature.

Types of Computerized Searches

- **Keyword** – *Unless you know the author or title of a book, keyword is the best type of search because it finds the search word or words anywhere in the bibliographical citation.*
  Example: water quality

- **Title** – **Type the exact order of words in the title.**
  Example: History of the United Kingdom

- **Author** – *Type the author's name, putting the last name first. You don't need to include a comma.*
  Example: Miller Henry J.

- **Subject** – *Type the exact Library of Congress subject heading.*
  Example: Spanish language – Grammar, Historical

- **Call Number** – *Type the exact call number.*
  Example: B851 .P49 2004

If you have a general topic, you probably want to use the key-word search. Subject search actually refers to the Library of Congress subject search designations, and, unless you use precisely the search terms specified by that classification system, you may not get the results you want. Using key words, however, will lead you to hits on your topic. Then, once you have found one book that is in your topic area, you can examine the screen for Library of Congress subject headings and click on those to browse for more books.

An invaluable resource of any library is the Interlibrary Loan Department. Here you can request books your library does not own, as well as journal articles from periodicals not in the library's collection or obtainable through the library's databases. The UCF-ILL Office can be accessed via the library homepage, where you can sign-up for an account. You can find more information about the UCF-ILL Office in the opening chapter of this book.

Use Electronic Library Resources

UCF's library increasingly relies on databases to provide digital versions of articles published in journals, magazines, newspapers, government documents, as well as other publications and materials. The databases are available to students and faculty through the Internet via the library home page. Your NID and NID password is required for off-campus access.

In keeping with the perspective that research is an iterative process, you will need to be aware that there are multiple databases you need to navigate. Some will be more useful for your particular topic than others. Database providers make choices about the content they will include in a variety of ways; one of these is by subject matter. Some databases will include journals on only a specific subject or a grouping of subjects. Knowing this, the UCF library provides a useful tool for students. By navigating to the UCF library's "Databases" page (visible in the screenshot below), you will be provided with subject specific links. Under each link a list of databases that seem well-suited for students researching in that field. For instance, clicking on the "Digital Media" link leads you to the databases "ACM Digital Library," "Communication & Mass Media Complete (Ebsco)," and "ERIC (Ebsco)," all databases that hold journals helpful to students studying digital media. On the databases page is also a list of popular databases used by UCF students.

Figure 2-4: Screenshot of databases

Database interfaces take on a variety of forms, but one common set-up for a database comes from the several that you might encounter that are provided by EBSCO. This database provider offers a variety of ways to search their databases, and their standard search interface appears similarly in all of their databases, much like the below screenshot of an "Academic Search Premier" search.

Figure 2-5: Screenshot of search interface

Library databases make use of online forms similar to those of a library computerized catalog. Searches are by subject, title, author, and name of publication. Advanced search features are available. Some databases provide full text of articles published in newspapers, journals, and magazines. Others give publication information only, such as title, author, publication, date of publication, and an abstract of the article. Popular databases include Lexis-Nexis, Academic Search Complete, Periodical Archive Online (Pro-Quest), Project Muse, and JSTOR.

Find Internet Information

The World Wide Web is an incredible resource for research. Through it, you can find full texts of pending legislation, searchable online editions of Shakespeare's plays, environmental impact statements, stock quotes, and much, much more. Finding credible research sources is not always easy. Anyone with an Internet connection and a little knowledge can put up a webpage and claim to be an expert on a chosen topic. Therefore, information from the Internet must be scrutinized with even more diligence than do print sources. For example, if you enter the word "environment" in one of the keyword search engines, you may receive thousands of "hits," or sites that relate to that topic from all over the world. How do you sift through all of that feedback in order to find information relevant to your topic? It is a problem that has not been completely solved on the Internet.

However, the search engine Google now provides Google Books, http://books.google.com, that offers full-text of millions of books, though usually not full-text of the entire book unless the book is no longer copy righted. Also, Google Scholar, http://scholar.google.com, provides access to scholarly papers, though if your library has computerized databases, it will likely have a more extensive collection available to you. The Directory of Online Open Access Journals, http://www.doaj.org, enables you to search online journals that offer free access.

Government Documents can also be found easily through the Internet and are indexed at a variety of sites, including these:

- FirstGov, http://www.firstgov.gov
- Thomas Legislative Information, http://thomas.loc.gov
- Federal Citizen Information Center, http://www.pueblo.gsa.gov/
- FedWorld.Gov, http://www.fedworld.gov/

One of the best ways for students to find Internet resources is through several indexing projects sponsored by major libraries. The UCF library provides excellent guides that can direct you toward useful search engines and electronic sources (including websites) in a variety of areas and fields. You can find them at guides.ucf. edu. It's a great place to begin your secondary research. An example of one of these research guides, "Digital Humanities" is shown on the following page.

Figure 2-6: Screenshot of UCF Libraries

Evaluate Sources

Many people tend to believe what they see in print. They may think that if information is in a book or a news magazine, it must be true. If you read critically, however, you know that all sources must be evaluated. With the Internet, perhaps even more than with print texts, it is important to evaluate your sources. Here are some guidelines to consider when evaluating sources.

- **Who is the author?** This question is equally important, whether the source in question is a book, a magazine, or a website. If you have the dust jacket of the book, the back flap will quickly provide you with essential information to screen the author. In the short biographical sketch, usually included along with a photo, you can learn the author's academic credentials and university affiliation, what previous books the author has published, and other qualification that the publisher thinks qualifies the author to write this particular book. If there is no dust jacket (as is often true with library books), you can try to find information about the author through an Internet search engine or a reference text such as *Contemporary Authors*. A magazine or journal will often provide brief biographical information at the end of the article or on a separate authors' page. If the text is on a website, determining the authorship is more complex, as authors often are not named. In that case, you are forced to rely on the credibility of the entity publishing the website. Many websites have a link called something like "About Us" or "Mission Statement," and that page will give you some idea about the motivations of the entity sponsoring the site. Are they selling something? Is it part of an organization that has a political agenda? These are things to keep in mind when considering the bias of the site's content.

- **For what audience is the text written?** Determining this may require some detective work. In the case of a book, the preface or introduction may give you some clues. With magazines and journals, consider the demographics of the readership. With a website, a little clicking around in the site should tell you from the kind of texts, graphics, and advertising (if any), what readers the site is designed for.

- **What sources does the author rely upon?** If you are working with an academic text, the sources should be clearly cited in the text by author and page number, footnotes, or endnotes. If it is a more popular book or article, sources are acknowledged less formally; however, a credible author will still make an effort to credit sources. For example, an article might say, "According to the March issue of the *New England Journal of Medicine*…."

- **Where does the author fit in the academic conversation?** Especially when looking for scholarly sources, you can think of how the author is responding to, extending, or using the work of other authors. They may be relying on academic sources, but sources that don't fit in your field's academic discussion. Also, the value of a source can depend on how seriously others in the field are taking it. If a source was published in 2012 and has only been cited once or twice by other authors, it might not be as valuable as a newer source that has been cited 15 or 20 times. *Web of Science* allows you to trace the number of times a source has been cited for most of the articles in its database. You can access this tool via the UCF library "Databases" page.

- **Does the text have an obvious bias?** Ask yourself if the argument is logical and if sources are mentioned for any statistics or other evidence. Are any opposing viewpoints discussed fairly? Does the author engage in name calling, a clear sign of bias? Are there obvious holes or contradictions in the argument? For most purposes, you are looking for texts which do not appear to have been written with a biased agenda. However, in some cases, the opposite is true. If you are looking for a political candidate's position on a certain issue, then reading the candidate's book or going to the candidate's website will provide you with a biased viewpoint but one which you can analyze for the purposes of your paper. When dealing with information from sources with an obvious agenda, though, you must be careful not to represent the material as unbiased in your text.

- **What do others think of the text?** For a book, you can look for a review in *Book Review Digest* or *Book Review Index*, two publications you can find in the reference section of the library. Also, the *New York Times* and other newspapers review prominent popular books. Most magazines and newspapers print letters to the editor which may offer comment on controversial articles. The Scout Report, which can be found at the *Scout Project*, http://scout.wisc.edu, reviews selected websites. If you locate a review of your text, you can cite the review in your research paper to provide additional evidence of the text's degree of credibility.

An Annotated Student Essay: "The Disinhibition of Reddit Users"

by Tiffany Gagnon
Produced in Adele Richardson's Spring 2013 ENC 1102

The culmination of research is the scholarly research article or essay. In UCF composition courses, students use the primary data and secondary sources they have gathered in order to make an effective argument about that contributes to an academic conversation. In this section, Tiffany Gagnon's "The Disinhibition of Reddit Users" is reproduced. Gagnon uses both primary and secondary research to make an effective argument about the environmental and community factors that lead to Reddit user disinhibition when communicating online. The text has been annotated—pay close attention to the comments in the margins; these point out the effective use of primary and secondary research data that Gagnon uses in her essay.

Introduction

1   There has been much research on the effects of anonymity in online communities and the disinhibition of its users. People experiencing online disinhibition act differently online than they would in offline settings (Chester and O'Hara 195, 197, 200-01; Lee 3; Suler "The Online" 321-24). Benign online disinhibition is characterized by the revealing of personal thoughts and showing unusual kindness (Suler "The Online" 321). Toxic online disinhibition describes disinhibited, harmful behavior that likely would not occur offline life (Lapidot-Lefler and Barak 434; Suler "The Online" 321). Disinhibited users are unlikely to "maintain accountability of identity"; however, it should be noted that disinhibition "does not necessarily lead to deceptive, dishonest, and fraudulent behavior" (Lee 3).

> Introduction sections establish the context for an essay. Sometimes, as in the case of Gagnon's text, they also review relevant secondary sources that will be used to support the author's argument. Other times, this review of sources is deployed in another section called the "Literature Review."

> Notice how Gagnon attributes this concept to multiple authors using a string citation. Doing so shows readers that the concept is generally accepted by the field and that it can operate as a starting point for the academic conversation.

> Using secondary sources effectively can mean placing ideas from authors in relation to each other. Gagnon associates two concepts as opposite categories of disinhibition, providing a fuller conception of the term for her readers. Throughout her introduction, Gagnon will continue to borrow ideas from various authors in a way that creatively frames her research.

2   Researchers recognize dissociative anonymity (a resistance to attach to offline identity) as the foundation of online disinhibition. It results in decreased feelings of vulnerability and increased self-disclosure and acting out (Lapidot-Lefler and Barak 435; Suler "The Online" 322). Noam Lapidot-Lefler and Azy Barak define anonymity as an "unidentifiability aspect...rather than namelessness," encompassing the concepts of pseudonymity and the withholding of identifying information (Lapidot-Lefler and Barak 435, 440-42). On another note, users that were surveyed in anonymous online communities feel that anonymity contributes

to negativity found in the forums, but a majority of users still support anonymity because they feel that it leads to more lively discussion (Rosenberry 12-13).

3   Invisibility is the inability to see physical responses from others while online that would ordinarily affect what people were to express in face-to-face settings (Lapidot-Lefler and Barak 435-36; Suler "The Online" 322-23). Asynchronicity also plays a role. When conversations are easily left and returned to, people do not have to deal with other's immediate responses (Suler "The Online" 322-23).

4   Rhetorical awareness is comprehension of one's purpose, motivations, audience, and the constraints on presenting discourse (Gee 489-90; Grant-Davie 106-11). The motivation is known as exigence; the rhetors are responsible for the discourse; the audience is who the discourse is intended for; and constraints are factors that hinder or help the discourse (Grant Davie 106-11). People recognize places of open online communication and may reveal private information even though they are aware of its public nature (Lee 3). James Paul Gee discusses metaknowledge in a rhetorical situation, "the ability to manipulate, analyze, [and] to resist while advancing" in the community, indicating rhetorical awareness and an understanding of a community's functions in order to advance within it (Gee 489-90).

> Many UCF composition students are required to frame their own research interests in the context of writing and rhetoric studies. The key is to make sure that this framing is a clear foundation of the research. Gagnon will draw on Gee, Grant-Davie, and Wardle, all authors usually assigned in UCF composition courses, to clearly position her argument as one that is valuable to writing and rhetoric scholars. The essay isn't just a report on disinhibition, but how anonymity online leads to rhetorical choices by disinhibited Reddit users.

5   People take on an identity in an environment usually by showing favorable parts of their personality (Suler "Identity" 457-58; Wardle 524-25). They can make the choice of who they are and may use this power towards self-actualization by practicing positive personality characteristics, while others may take on a harmful identity (Suler "Identity" 457-58). There are also users who want to "receive and not show too much" by engaging in lurking behaviors by simply observing the community (Suler "Identity" 456, 459). Elizabeth Wardle argues that users construct their identities through their rhetorical choices, writing in ways that are appropriate in the community to help establish a positive social identity (Wardle 525).

6   Suler and Grant-Davie have done excellent jobs at explaining online disinhibition and rhetorical situation, respectively, and there have been many studies conducted to explain the disinhibition in different communities. However, I would like to build on these studies with my own on the disinhibition of users within a popular social media website: Reddit. My research focuses on the evidence of online disinhibition displayed in posted content resulting from the anonymity of Reddit users.

> This is one of Gagnon's most important paragraphs. She first establishes what work has been accomplished by previous scholars. Then, she positions her own essay as an extension of these authors' ideas by situating her research in the particular context of Reddit. Remember, academic writers need to clearly be engaged in academic conversations. Here, Gagnon shows she has listened to what others have said about disinhibition and rhetoric and will now argue for her own, new position.

Methodology

7   As a Reddit visitor for two years, I am quite familiar with the site and believed that this environment could be valuable to the discussion on online disinhibition. To observe Reddit for the presence of this effect, I developed the following research question:

> The methodology section of a scholarly essay is where the author details their primary research methods so that they can be scrutinized and possibly replicated.

8   How do Reddit's users embrace and take advantage of their anonymity within the site?

> Gagnon's research questions is contextualized, answerable, and potentially valuable to other writing and rhetoric scholars.

9   From there, my research took on the role of digital discourse community ethnography, and comprehending the basic workings of Reddit is crucial to understanding how users can interact on the site.

10   This social media site is coined "the front page of the Internet." Current news and entertainment found on the web quickly end up on Reddit. The site functions through its registered users who submit content while others vote to rank how high it appears on the page. Registered users can also leave comments on posts. Anyone can access Reddit, but only the registered users may submit, comment, and vote. They can also create and subscribe to subreddits—subcommunities—of Reddit that discuss a specific topic. Registration does not require any information about offline identity

11   I observed popular subreddits as well as the discussion surrounding controversial topics involving Reddit. I used notecards to record my observations and bookmarked links back to my observed content's original source. Data was collected over a two-week period from topics on Reddit and comment threads. Several comments from users were recorded; however, usernames were not recorded for the sake of privacy.

> Which of the primary research methods in the previous section involve the observation of people in a community with as little impact on the community as possible? Ethnography! Gagnon uses ethnographic research in order to collect important data for her argument.

12   I did note if a user was clearly using a "throwaway" account, an account created to dissociate a comment from one's usual Reddit username. I determined a throwaway account from a main account by these criteria:

1. The account history contains only the comment related to it.

2. The username contains the word "throwaway" or is directly related to the content of the observed comment.

13   For a section of my study, I focus on one user in particular: Michael Brutsch, pseudonym violentacrez, because of his harmful behavior on Reddit that became known to the offline public. He is not currently an active member of Reddit, as he was banned last year, but he has he had a lasting impact on the community.

> Gagnon reveals her additional use of case study methods to offer readers an in-depth look at this famous Reddit user.

14   I examined my data for instances of online disinhibition. I considered the factors that are playing a role in the disinhibition that Reddit users can experience.

I recognized the rhetorical situations of individual content by considering what subreddit the content had been posted in, its purpose, and the audience. My presence during discussion was not known; therefore, it was not possible for users to feel a need to adjust their behavior as a result of my observation.

Results and Discussion

> The "Results" and "Discussion" sections, sometimes combined as by Gagnon, show the collected data and discuss how that data leads to and supports authorial claims, respectively.

Ask Reddit: Spill Your Life to Strangers

15   The subreddit *Ask Reddit* is a community where users may pose thought-provoking questions to discuss. While observing some of the top discussions, I found this very popular topic: "Throwaway time! What's your secret that could literally ruin your life if it came out?" "Throwaway" refers to the "throwaway accounts" I described. The following are responses to this thread written under throwaway accounts:

1. "I once helped out my female friend's family by taking care of their cat for a week…. I would snoop around their house. I found my friend's diary, and read the entire thing. I used this information to get her to like me, and she is currently my wife."
2. "When I was 13, I was molested by a guy who dragged me into an alley…. My friend doesn't believe me. I've never told anyone because I don't want them to react the way my 'friend' did."
3. "I faked the last two years of college."
4. "Everyone thinks I have a good job and roommates but I've been homeless and a prostitute for over a year."

16   These Reddit users are using this confession thread as a place to share secrets that are weighing on them. Throwaway accounts are an example of a Reddit user's power over their anonymity. They can make the choice to dissociate from their Reddit identity further by simply using an alternate pseudonym and then leaving it behind. This dissociative anonymity allows them to feel more willing to self-disclose with the community (Suler "The Online" 322). They

> In these sentences, Gagnon effectively transitions from the reporting of data to making an argument based on that data. Notice how her argument "Throwaway accounts are an example of Reddit user's power over their anonymity" is supported by Suler's conclusions about how online users become disinhibited.

can share their secret and walk away from any further discussion, as the conversation is asynchronous. No immediate reactions from others have to be dealt with, and the conversation can be resumed whenever the user decides, if at all (Suler "The Online" 322-23). For instance, in comment 2, the user clearly expresses that (s)he has never told anyone else about the incident, but the comment discloses it to anyone who reads it. Even though the user is discussing the secret publicly, invisibility and asynchronous conversation allow the user to leave the conversation freely. Anyone who posts a secret does not worry about

> Looking for expert argument construction? Check this out. Earlier in the paragraph, Gagnon offered a few claims based on the data she gathered. In these lines, she defends her position by clearly analyzing one specific piece of her ethnographic data. When your instructors say "Show, don't tell," this is what they mean.

eye contact with the people they are telling, and physical signs of disapproval are not there to inhibit what the user is willing to share (Suler "The Online" 322). Creation of throwaway accounts demonstrates the rhetorical awareness of the users creating them: they understand the purpose of the thread is not to be able to identify anyone based on their response, but to provide shocking confessions for entertainment. The four users behind comments 1-4 recognize that their usual Reddit pseudonym is not important or relevant. This metaknowledge gives them an advantage with authority over their anonymity (Gee 489-90). Understanding that it is acceptable to create an account to simply ditch it once it serves its purpose allows users to resist singlepseudonym conformity and advance in discussion in the community. The user is aware that they are the rhetor behind the comment, and therefore serve as its authorial voice (Grant-Davie 108). Audience can influence what identity the user—the rhetor—will assume, but when it is possible to remain anonymous, the user may consider the audience's presence much less than in an identifying situation.

> In this paragraph, Gagnon's ethnographic research methodology requires textual analysis. She draws conclusions based on what people have written on the Reddit feed.

17   Pseudonyms allow Reddit users to be more honest about themselves in their comments. Andrea Chester and Agi O'Hara also found that the students in their study using pseudonyms claimed to do so to be more honest (Chester and O'Hara 200). Even though Reddit is public, the discussions such as the confessions listed above still appear on the site. Disclosing private information has been found to occur in public online settings when pseudonyms allow for a lack of accountability (Lee 2-3). Users are unlikely to be worried that their confession comments will affect them in their offline life.

> At the end of several sections, Gagnon deploys a paragraph that ties the section's argument to her overall exploration of disinhibited Reddit users. An expert rhetorical move, these paragraphs serve to remind readers of the overall message of the cohesive essay.

Gone Wild: Show Your Body to Reddit

> In this section, Gagnon analyzes the visual elements of the "Gone Wild" Reddit, drawing on elements of the multimodal text analysis research method.

18   Gone Wild is a subreddit described as a place for adults to post pictures of their nude bodies. By reviewing account histories, I observed that a majority of the users post their pictures from an account that is not associated with other parts of Reddit. Furthermore, most photos I observed did not contain a face, or faces were at least partially hidden. Titles for posted photos are usually flirty and provocative.

19   Gone Wild allows its posters to create an identity driven by sexual attraction, while   dissociating from their offline identity as well as their usual Reddit identity if an alternate account is being used. Creating a Gone Wild identity can be a person's way of attaining a "new, idealized way of being" (Suler "Identity" 457). They may be fulfilling a self-esteem or self-expression need. Those wishing to successfully create an identity on Gone Wild must follow a

> Notice Gagnon's continued use of framing concepts offered by Suler. Gagnon is following through with the promise she made in her introduction—she's extending the academic conversation by applying Suler's concepts in a particular context.

specific way of writing and presenting themselves in the community. Members of a community must be comfortable with writing and rhetorical conventions of the community (Wardle 524-25). Failing to provide the types of photos that viewers are looking for on Gone Wild will cause the user to fail to achieve a positive identity among the community. In addition, failing to produce flirtatious titles and descriptions can minimize the authority of the user among viewers.

> In addition to the disinhibition frameworks provided by Suler, Gagnon effectively relies on writing and rhetoric scholars to explore the rhetorical choices of Reddit users. Here, Wardle helps her understand the genre standards of the Gone Wild community.

20   Withholding offline identity on *Gone Wild* by hiding identifying features indicates that the user is aware of the context of the community, and the consequences that could be faced in offline life if identity is revealed. It is clear that they wish to remain anonymous when they have hidden their face from camera's view, and some users will black out any obvious identifying features, such as tattoos, as necessary. Attempts at separating their online actions from their offline identity leads to the dissociative anonymity that gives many users the courage to post their photos.

Random Acts of Benign Disinhibition

21   There are many subreddits that use a variation of the name *Random Acts of...* to identify the community as a place for requesting, exchanging, and helping out others in need of something specific. An example is *Random Acts of Christmas*. During the holiday season, users can make requests for and offer holiday gifts for children when parents are faced with difficult financial times. When searching through posts about last holiday season, I found a parent graciously thanking the community for their help:

22   "So remember all those books y'all sent my little girls?! Well, I'd like to hug you all again and say another big THANK YOU.... [M]y daughter's school just called me and said...her reading average has improved from a 70 to a 92! I know it's because of all the extra reading she's been doing!"

23   The kindness and generosity seen in these Random Act communities can be described as benign online disinhibition (Suler "The Online" 321). This is not to say that the generous Reddit users are unkind in their offline lives, but to imply that they take advantage of these opportunities to make a difference in someone's life that they may not have been able to otherwise. Moreover, in offline life, people can be shy to offer their help to others. These subreddits allow an anonymous way to affect a stranger's life positively. Expressing generosity online can be an opportunity to practice positive character traits and help in accomplishing self-actualization (Suler "The Online" 457).

Misinterpreting Anonymity: The Applebee's Waitress and the Google Employee

> Part of ethnographic research can include historical research. In this section, Gagnon is able to draw on researched history of the Reddit community in order to make an argument about online disinhibition. She uses the history of two particular cases as her researched data.

24   In February 2013, a waitress posted in the subreddit *Atheism* a picture of a check she found both insulting and amusing. For the "tip" section of the check, the customer, whom the waitress identified as a pastor, wrote, "I give God 10%, why do you get 18%?" and left the waitress without a tip. The photo and story went viral and according to news posted to Reddit, the waitress was soon identified as "Chelsea" and the pastor as "Ms. Bell." Chelsea reported that she "withheld any identifying information" in her Reddit post and that she "posted the note as a lighthearted joke," After her exposure, Applebee's reportedly fired her for exposing the customer's check and signature.

25   A similar story involves a Google employee hired as a "Chrome Specialist" who enthusiastically posted a photo of his new work uniform on Reddit. In the thread, he mentioned that he had been trained to promote the Chromebook computer in stores such as Best Buy. His post and mention of his training violated the nondisclosure agreement he had with Google, and Google identified and fired him.

26   Chelsea did not expect to lose her job by posting the photo of the check on Reddit. She is a victim of misinterpreting her anonymity on Reddit. She failed to remain anonymous or develop the rhetorical awareness necessary to see the possible consequences of her actions. She once had the authority as the rhetor behind the posted photo and description, but her audience that was responsible for her exposure caused her to lose that authorial voice (Grant-Davie 108-10). As result, her post easily backfired on her.

27   The ex-Google employee also lost his authority as the rhetor. The photo he posted quickly led to an interesting discussion thread, but when it was exposed that he was being fired over the Reddit post and violation of his nondisclosure agreement, opinion of him quickly turned sour. Reddit users commented how ignorant he was to have so easily violated his agreement with Google. He went from having an identity as an interesting new Google employee to being the misinformed man who made a poor decision that cost him his job. In developing an online identity, he did not maintain offline accountability for his actions or take into account how public they were (Lee 3).

Violentacrez: An Exposed Case of Toxic Disinhibition

28   *Violentacrez* is the online pseudonym behind a now-banned Reddit account of 49 year-old Michael Brutsch. On Reddit, Brutsch had created many distasteful subreddits, some which still remain today. He was banned from Reddit in October 2012 and his identity had been revealed by Gawker.com, later followed by his interview with CNN. Brutsch's employer fired him shortly following his exposure (Roy).

29   An example of a subreddit created by *violentacrez* is "Jailbait," a place for photos of eye-catching underage girls. The subreddit is now banned because of obvious controversy that arose, but many of *violentacrez's* other subreddits remain. *Pics*

of Dead Kids is a subreddit that still remains, albeit it is not very active. The title is to the point: users may post pictures found on the Internet—usually very gory—of dead children. It is an unsettling community filled with appalling pictures and comments, but it represents the freedom expressed online and the types of things people may view or post when they are hidden behind a computer screen

30   Brutsch admits he "didn't really think" about what he was doing on Reddit, and he referred to his username in the third-person during his CNN interview. He also expressed regret over the interview in the first place (Roy). This displays his dissociation with his online identity, violentacrez, from his offline identity, because he went as far as referring to his username as if it was not himself behind that identity. Brutsch visited dark territory of the internet—and created it—but has not been proven to explore such territory in his offline life. I knew of his existence on Reddit when his account had yet to be banned. He had achieved an identity described as "the creepy uncle of Reddit," which was almost humorous without looking into his account activity. Reddit did not take action to ban this user until the controversy led to exposure of his offline identity.

> Gagnon uses historical data in this paragraph as well, this time drawing on a CNN interview. Analysis of language use in the interview leads Gagnon to draw useful conclusions about online disinhibition through disassociation with offline identity. Writing and rhetoric scholars pay close attention to language choices when analyzing primary research data (see Lissa Pompos' handout on "Ways to Look for 'Themes' or Recurring Ideas in Your Primary, Qualitative Data" in this research chapter).

31   It is likely that Brutsch had been releasing a negative aspect of his psyche into a world— Reddit—in which he did not think it could be associated with his offline identity (Suler "Identity" 457). He catered to a shock-value oriented audience, with an exigence of jolting users of Reddit and creating a famous negative identity for himself.

Lurkers: You Can't See Me

32   Lurkers are the users of Reddit who do not participate in discussion and do not make their presence known. They want to "receive and not show too much" (Suler "Identity" 459). I define them as unregistered users, or registered users who participate in discussion rarely or never. Throughout this study and my usual browsing of Reddit, I've been a lurker.

33   I lurk on Reddit to be entertained in times of boredom. It also serves as a place to fuel my procrastination. As much as I take from Reddit and as much as it offers me, I do not give back very much; however, I do not feel much guilt about it. I am invisible on Reddit—no one is judging me personally on my lack of contribution to the community because no one can see me. In a similar situation in offline life, I would feel more compelled to contribute to a cause if I was around people who are. But in an online setting such as Reddit, I can satisfy my need to separate my personal identity from my observation of those around me (Suler "Identity" 459).

Conclusion

34   Reddit is a community where online disinhibition can be found throughout, but no published study on disinhibition pertaining to

> Conclusion sections of research essays often recap the argument the author made in the whole of the essay, connect the research to larger academic discussions, and/or call for further studies.

Reddit users exists. My findings are a work in progress—to help narrow the gap on what we understand about the disinhibition resulting from the pseudonymous nature of Reddit. They

> Gagnon expresses a realistic understanding of the impact of her claims, treating them as a useful starting point in a larger academic conversation and setting up a call for further research.

indicate the presence of this behavior in yet another popular online environment, and point to Reddit as a source for further valuable research. The results of this study contribute to the discussion on online communities where disinhibition has been observed.

35   This study needs to be followed by other discussion of the psychology behind Reddit. As popular a site as Reddit is, more research needs to be done to understand the interactions that occur within it. Other pseudonymous online communities should be studied for disinhibition in comparison to findings about Reddit. It is crucial to understand what factors of pseudonymous communities can affect the disinhibition and behavior of its users.

> Gagnon specifies her call for further research, arguing for the necessity of such research while again supplementing the value of her own study.

36   The Internet and social media play a huge role in many people's lives today. Understanding the workings behind the socialization and how its users choose to present themselves is vital in order to fully understand why these websites captivate us so much. To understand the behavior of users of these sites is to further understand human nature. Humans act variably in face-to-face situations, but online interaction pushes people into a rhetorical situation unlike any other. Understanding behavior in these contexts can lead to discussion on the "true self" of a person, and if it even exists at all. Online disinhibition is a phenomenon that represents more than a deviation from an offline identity. It illustrates the ability of the human mind to adapt and create fluctuating identities dependent on context and experience.

> In these concluding sentences, Gagnon successfully ties her research to larger academic conversations.

Works Cited

Chester, Andrea, and Agi O'Hara. "Image, Identity and Pseudonymity In Online Discussions." *International Journal of Learning* 13.12 (2007): 193-203. *Education Source*. Web. 3 Feb. 2013.

Gee, James Paul. "Literacy, Discourse, and Linguistics: Introduction." Wardle and Downs 482-95.

Grant-Davie, Keith. "Rhetorical Situations and Their Constituents." Wardle and Downs 104-18.

Lapidot-Lefler, Noam, and Azy Barak. "Effects Of Anonymity, Invisibility, and Lack of Eye-Contact on Toxic Online Disinhibition." *Computers in Human Behavior* 28.2 (2012): 434-43. Social Sciences Citation Index. Web. 3 Feb. 2013.

Lee, Hangwoo. "Privacy, Publicity, and Accountability of Self-Presentation in an On-Line Discussion Group." *Sociological Inquiry* 76.1 (2006): 1-22. *Academic Search Premier*. Web. 3 Feb. 2013.

Rosenberry, Jack. "Users Support Online Anonymity Despite Increasing Negativity." *Newspaper Research Journal* 32.2 (2011): 6-19. OmniFile Full Text Mega. Web. 27 Feb. 2013.

Roy, Jessica. "Violentacrez Admits Doing CNN Interview Was a 'Huge Mistake.'" *Betabeat*. Observer Media Group, 19 Oct. 2012. Web. 2 Mar. 2013.

Suler, John. "Identity Management in Cyberspace." *Journal of Applied Psychoanalytic Studies* 4.4 (2002): 455-59. PsycINFO. Web. 3 Feb. 2013.

Suler, John. "The Online Disinhibition Effect." *CyberPsychology & Behavior* 7.3 (2004): 321- 26. Academic Search Premier. Web. 3 Feb. 2013.

Wardle, Elizabeth. "Identity, Authority, and Learning to Write in New Workplaces." Wardle and Downs 521-35.

Wardle, Elizabeth, and Doug Downs, eds. *Writing about Writing: A College Reader*. Boston: Bedford/St. Martin's, 2011.

CHAPTER 3

Citation

Edited by Lissa Pompos Mansfield

Why Should I Cite Sources?

Chances are, you already have some experience with citing sources. When you wrote a research paper for your high school English class, for example, you were probably expected to find sources that supported your argument; integrate quotes, paraphrases, and summaries from those sources into your prose; and then show your reader where you got that information from. If you have ever written a Bibliography, Works Cited, or list of References, you have practiced citing your sources.

When you write for your college courses, the expectations for these citations will differ depending on the academic discipline of the class. For example, if your psychology professor asks you to create a lab report, they will probably ask you to follow APA (American Psychological Association) formatting guidelines. However, if your writing professor asks you to complete a literature review on a topic, they will probably ask you to follow MLA (Modern Language Association) formatting guidelines. This is one example of why citing is important: it helps you to show your knowledge of disciplinary writing conventions.

There are lots of other reasons why you, as a writer and researcher, should cite your sources. Citing allows you to establish your ethos and gain the trust of your audience, provide context for the conversation around your topic, help your readers locate sources, acknowledge other writers, and avoid plagiarism.

To Establish Your Ethos

As a writer, you have many responsibilities to fulfill for your readers, such as: keeping the needs of your audience in mind when making decisions about word choice, the amount and types of examples you include, and the organization and presentation of your argument; verifying and presenting the most accurate information you can about your topic; and establishing your ethos.

Ethos refers to the writer's (or speaker's) credibility. An ancient Greek philosopher named Aristotle described ethos, one of the three artistic appeals, as a proof that "reside[s] in the character of the speaker." In other words, ethos encompasses all the parts of your argument where you persuade your audience that you are a person of good character and credibility.

An important way that you can establish your ethos is by properly citing your sources. By using appropriate sources (e.g., peer-reviewed scholarly journal articles that are published in reputable journals or books that are often cited by other writers in your field of study), you demonstrate that you have done your homework and can be trusted to provide current and relevant information. By citing your sources, you demonstrate that you are honest and credible.

However, there are many different citation styles, such as MLA (Modern Language Association), APA (American Psychological Association), and CMS (Chicago Manual of Style), you can choose from when you cite. To maintain your ethos, it is important to adhere to the citation standards for your discipline. If you ever wonder what type of citation style you should use for a specific writing task, it is always wise to ask your instructor or look at examples written by other authors in your field of study.

To Provide Context

Another reason why writers include citations is to provide context. Writers don't write in a vacuum—they are always constrained by the ***rhetorical situation*** they are writing in and they are usually responding to an ongoing conversation about their topic. When you cite a source, you are positioning that author within a larger conversation.

Each source you cite represents a separate "voice" in the conversation about your topic. Part of your job as a writer is to show the reader how those voices are responding to one another. In other words, you are helping readers draw connections between authors' theories and concepts. Your readers probably do not know as much about your topic as you do, so you need to provide clues about whose voices matter in the conversation. Citing helps you to do this because citations emphasize where you are getting your ideas from.

To Help Others Locate Sources

Have you ever read an article that contained a reference to another source that intrigued you? Have you ever found a perfect source for your research paper while skimming another source? If you have experienced either of these moments, you know that citations can provide a lot of useful information for finding other great pieces of writing.

To help your readers find sources, you need to give them clues about the source's location. Think about your list of citations as a "map" that points readers to the books, journals, websites, and databases they want to find. Each entry, or full citation, gives you the exact "address" of a source. For example, the citation for an article in an online journal will include not only the name of the journal (to continue the metaphor of an address, the journal would be similar to a neighborhood), but also the volume and issue number (the cross streets or intersection of a house), the title (the house number) and the authors' names (the occupants). An **in-text citation** in the body text of a piece is like a landmark or checkpoint on the map—it gives you a reference point you can use when consulting your map (for writers who use MLA style citations, this is the ***Works Cited***, and for writers who use APA style citations, this is the list of ***References***). When you include citations, you provide your readers with all the information they need to locate sources they want to find.

To Acknowledge Other Writers

As a writer and researcher, you need to give credit where credit is due. Authors work hard to produce the articles, books, webpages, videos, handouts, and other texts we read. These original creations are considered the author's ***intellectual property***. Intellectual property refers to "creations of the mind, such as inventions, literary and artistic works, designs and symbols, [and] names and images used in commerce" (WIPO). Intellectual property includes the subcategories of patents, copyrights, trademarks, and trade secrets (Cornell University Law School). When you cite a source, you acknowledge the author of that source and make sure others know who created that text.

To Avoid Plagiarism

As discussed in previous paragraphs, when you cite your sources, you are showing your readers who wrote a text and where it can be found. You are also giving authors credit for their ideas and language. When writers do not give proper credit for their sources, they may be guilty of plagiarism or misuse of sources.

The UCF DWR adopted the following definition of ***plagiarism*** from the Council of Writing Program Administrators (WPA):

> In an instructional setting, plagiarism occurs when a writer deliberately uses someone else's language, ideas, or other original (not common-knowledge) material without acknowledging its source. This definition applies to texts published in print or online, to manuscripts, and to the work of other student writers.

The WPA also defines the ***misuse of sources***:

> A student who attempts (even if clumsily) to identify and credit his or her source, but who misuses a specific citation format or incorrectly uses

quotation marks or other forms of identifying material taken from other sources, has not plagiarized. Instead, such a student should be considered to have failed to cite and document sources appropriately.

By including in-text citations and full citation entries in your paper, you demonstrate a good faith effort in crediting your sources.

When Should I Cite Sources?

Throughout your academic career, you will be exposed to many **genres** that use citations, such as scholarly journal articles, research papers, annotated bibliographies, and the like. While it is important to know, in general, that citations should be used in these types of texts, it is also important to recognize the different ways citations get used. Some common moments when writers use citations include after summarizing, paraphrasing, or quoting a source.

There are also two categories of citations you will often use when writing for a college class: an in-text citation and a full citation. An **in-text citation** (also known as a **parenthetical citation**) is a citation that appears in the body text of a piece of writing and corresponds with the full citation found in the Works Cited or References section. In-text citations point readers to where they can find more information about your source. A **full citation** contains all the information your reader would need to know to locate the original source (e.g., author, title, publication venue, medium of publication, etc.).

Using accurate in-text citations helps guide your reader to the appropriate entry on the Works Cited. For example, the in-text citation given below in parentheses directs the reader to the correct page of the book given in the Works Cited.

In-text Citation:
When a teenager sleeps more than 10 hours per night, it is time to question whether she is having significant problems (Jones 63).

Entry in Works Cited:
Jones, Stephanie. *The Signs of Trouble*. Boston: Dilemma Publishing, 2010. Print.

Summarizing, Paraphrasing, or Quoting a Source

There are three main ways that you can include ideas or language from a source in your writing—you can summarize, paraphrase, or quote the material (Driscoll and Brizee). In each of these cases, you need to cite your source(s) to show where the ideas or language originated.

"What are the differences among quoting, paraphrasing, and summarizing sources?" you might be wondering. When you quote a source, you are using exact language and phrasing from the source. To quote correctly, you need to put this language in quotation marks AND give credit to the source (e.g., using an in-text citation). You might want to use direct quotation when the wording or structure of a phrase is noteworthy and/or cannot be paraphrased without losing its intended meaning, tone, or effect.

When you paraphrase a source, you are putting the language and ideas of a source in your own words. You might want to paraphrase a source when the idea of a phrase is important, but you would like to simplify the vocabulary or complexity of the passage. To paraphrase correctly, you need to give credit to the source (e.g., using an in-text citation).

Like a paraphrase, when you summarize a source, you are putting the language and ideas of a source in your own words, but in this case, you are significantly condensing those ideas. Summaries only contain the most important and relevant points of the passage; minor details and examples are often excluded. To summarize correctly, you need to give credit to the source (e.g., using an in-text citation).

See the section titled "In-Text Citations" for models and explanations of how to create an in-text citation for a summary, paraphrase, or direct quotation of another source.

Distinguishing Between Works Cited and Works Consulted

While the format of a Works Cited and a Works Consulted is very similar, they differ in terms of the content included. In a **Works Cited**, you list all the sources you cited in your text. In a **Works Consulted**, you list both the sources you cited in your text and the sources you read or "consulted" when preparing your text.

So, how do you know when to create a Works Consulted or a Works Cited? Depending on how you're using sources, you might create just a Works Consulted, just a Works Cited, or both. If you are reading sources for background information and you are not including any quotes or in-text citations for those sources in your paper, create a list of Works Consulted. If you are quoting, paraphrasing, or summarizing sources, you need to include full citations for them in your Works Cited. If your paper used both "consulted" and "cited" sources, you might choose to create both Works Consulted and Works Cited pages. For examples, see the end of this chapter.

How Should I Cite Sources?

This handbook covers two of the most common citation styles students are asked to use when writing at the University of Central Florida: MLA and APA.

Citing in MLA Format

If you write in composition, language, linguistics, and literature courses, you will often be asked to use documentation guidelines created by the Modern Language Association (MLA). The *MLA Handbook for Writers of Research Papers*, in its eighth edition, provides a full description of the conventions used by this

particular community of writers; updates to the *MLA Handbook* can be found at www.mla.org.

Another great citation reference is provided by the Purdue OWL Writing Lab. Their online *MLA Formatting and Style Guide* is available at https://owl.english.purdue.edu/owl/resource/747/1/.

MLA guidelines require that you give both an in-text citation and a Works Cited entry for any and all sources you use.

Did You Know?

The Modern Language Association was founded in 1883 at The John Hopkins University as a group that discussed literature and modern languages, such as Spanish, French, Chinese, and English. The MLA, now with over 30,000 members in over 100 countries, is the primary professional association for literature and language scholars.

In-Text Citations

When you use MLA documentation style, you need to indicate the author's last name and the location of the source material (page or paragraph number). Where this in-text information is placed depends on how you want to phrase the sentence that is summarized, paraphrased, or quoted. Be sure that the in-text citation guides the reader clearly to the source in the Works Cited, where complete information about the source is given.

The following are some of the most common examples of parenthetical citations.

Author's name in text

When using a parenthetical reference to a single source that is already named in the sentence, use this form: (Page number). Note that the period goes after the parentheses.

Stephanie Jones, author of *The Signs of Trouble*, describes "excessive sleeping, refraining from eating, and lying about simple things" as signs to look for when parents are concerned about their children (63).

Author's name in reference

When the author's name is not included in the preceding sentence, use this form for the parenthetical information at the end of the sentence: (Author's Last Name Page number). Note that there is no comma between the name and page in an MLA parenthetical reference, and also note that the period comes at the end of the sentence after the parentheses.

When a teenager sleeps more than 10 hours per night, it is time to question whether she is having significant problems (Jones 63).

No author given

When a work has no credited author, use a clipped version of the work's title.

In a recent *Time* article, a list of 30 common signs of teenage trouble cites lack of sleep as the most common sign ("Thirty" 3).

Two authors given

When you use a source that was written by two authors, use both authors' names in the text of the sentence or in the citation.

The idea that "complexity is a constant in biology" is not an innovative one (Sole and Goodwin 2).

Three or more authors given

When you use a source written by three or more authors, include only the first author's name followed by et al. (Latin for "and others").

In Hong Kong, most signs are in Chinese and English; however, once you are in mainland China, English is rarely found on signs, except in tourist areas (Li, et al. 49).

Authors with the same last names

If your source material includes items by authors who have the same last name, use each author's first initial in the parentheses. If the two authors also share first initials, use one of the authors' full first names.

When a teenager sleeps more than 10 hours per night, it is time to question whether she is having significant problems (S. Jones 63).

Another sign of trouble can be when you do not see your child for meals (Sally Jones 114).

Encyclopedia or dictionary unsigned entry

When you use an encyclopedia or dictionary to look up a word or entry, be sure to include the word or entry title in the parenthetical entry.

The word *thing* has more definitions than any other entry in the *Oxford English Dictionary* ("thing").

Lines of verse (plays, poetry or song lyrics)

When citing plays, give the act, scene, and line numbers of the material you use. Separate the act, scene, and line numbers with periods. For example, the quotation below comes from *Romeo and Juliet*, Act II, Scene 2, lines 43 and 44. The MLA also advises using this method with biblical chapters and verses. Be sure, though, that the sequence goes from largest unit to smallest unit.

Juliet grapples with how names can influence feelings as she questions, "What's in a name? That which we call a rose/By any other name would smell as sweet" (2.2.43-44).

Use a slash (/) to signify line breaks when you quote poetry or song lyrics, and put line numbers in the in-text citation instead of page numbers.

> An early song by Will Smith shows the frustration of children as he sings, "You know parents are the same/No matter time nor place/They don't understand that us kids/Are going to make some mistakes" (1-4).

Indirect quotation

Sometimes, while reading a text such as a journal article, you come across a quote or source that is cited in the article you're reading that you'd also like to quote in your writing. When you cite a source that is cited in another source it is considered an **indirect source** (Russell et al., "MLA In-Text Citations: The Basics"). To attribute credit to the source you actually used, use "qtd. in." for MLA format and "as cited in" for APA format. When you use a quotation of a quotation—that is, a quotation that quotes from another source—use qtd. in to designate the source. For example:

> Swales lists six criteria that a group must meet to be considered a discourse community, which includes having "a broadly agreed set of common public goals" (qtd. in Johns 500).
>
> Swales lists six criteria that a group must meet to be considered a discourse community, which includes having "a broadly agreed set of common public goals" (as cited in Johns, 1997, p. 500).
>
> Smith has said, "My parents really didn't understand me" (qtd. in Jones 8).

Using Long or Block Quotations

Long or block quotations have special formatting requirements of their own.

Block quote of prose

If you quote a chunk of prose that is longer than four typed lines, you are using what is called a **block quotation**. Follow these MLA guidelines for block quotations:

- If introducing the block quotation with a sentence, use a colon at the end of the sentence. If the introduction to your block quote is not a complete sentence, use whatever punctuation is appropriate to connect the introduction to the quote. If there is no grammatical need for punctuation, do not use any.
- Begin the quotation on a new line.
- Do not use quotation marks to enclose the block quote.
- Indent the quote one half inch from the left margin.
- Double space the entire quotation.
- Put a period at the end of the quotation, and then add the parenthetical citation.

> However, Lansky states:
>
> Despite the statement on www.signspotting.com that we don't accept signs with the intention of being funny, people like sending them in. I've opted not to use these as it could encourage people to start making them, sticking them up in their driveway, and snapping a picture. Plus, funny signs are so much more amusing when the humor is accidental. (72)

See that introduction to the quote above, where the author writes "However, Lansky states" before the block quotation? That is an example of a **signal phrase**. Signal phrases are used to indicate that a quote will soon be included. Often, signal phrases include some information about the source, such as the author of the quote or the title of the piece where the quote appears. Using the example above, we can see that the signal phrase includes information about the author, Lansky. Another common feature of signal phrases is the presence of a signal verb. In the example above, we see that Lansky *states*.

If you search the web for signal phrases, you can probably find lots of templates and examples to use in your paper. Some common signal phrases and verbs are listed below:

- Author X states "insert quotation here."
- As claimed by Author X, "insert quotation here."
- Author X agrees with Author Y by saying "insert quotation here."

Here are some verbs that you can use in your signal phrases: acknowledges, adds, admits, affirms, agrees, answers, argues, asks, asserts, attacks, believes, calls, claims, comments, compares, concedes, confirms, contends, counters, declares, defines, denies, disputes, echoes, emphasizes, finds, implies, insinuates, insists, labels, mentions, notes, observes, points out, predicts, proposes, reasons, recognizes, recommends, refutes, rejects, reports, responds, reveals, says, speculates, states, suggests, tells, thinks, warns, and writes ("Verbs Used in MLA Style Signal Phrases").

Block quote of poetry, drama, or song lyrics

For songs and poems, be sure to give line numbers rather than page numbers and to use the original line breaks.

The Fresh Prince, an early Will Smith character, sings about parents not understanding:

> You know parents are the same No matter time or place They don't understand that us kids Are going to make some mistakes So to you other kids all across the land There's no need to argue Parents just don't understand. (4-7)

Adding or Omitting Words in a Quotation

Adding words to a quotation

Use square brackets ([ ]) to point out words or phrases that you have added to clarify or add context to your quotation but are not part of the original text.

> Original quotation: "When we entered the People's Republic of China, we noticed that the signage began dropping English translations."

> Quotation with added word: She said," When we entered the People's Republic of China, [Dunkirk and I] noticed that the signage began dropping English translations" (Donelson 141).

You can also add your own comments inside a quotation by using square brackets. For example, you can add the word *sic* to a quotation when you know that there is an error.

Sic is a Latin adverb (literally: sic erat scriptum) that means "thus was it written." According to Wikipedia, when sic follows a quoted word or passage, that means "the quoted matter has been transcribed exactly as found in the source text, complete with any erroneous or archaic spelling, surprising assertion, faulty reasoning, or other matter that might otherwise be taken as an error of transcription" ("Sic"). A writer might include sic in a quoted passage to show that they are aware of the error but they have chosen to retain the original language. A common example would be using sic in a quotation that uses the word "men" to stand in for all people (including women). Some writers will use sic to draw attention to this sexist word or phrase. For instance:

Edmund Burke asserted "Example is the school of mankind [sic], and they will learn at no other."

Original quotation: "When we entered the People's Repulic of China, we noticed that the signage began dropping English translations."

Quotation with added comment: She said, "When we entered the People's Repulic [sic] of China, we noticed that the signage began dropping English translations" (Donelson 141).

Omitting words in a quotation

Use an ellipsis (…) to represent words, phrases, or sentences that you delete from a quotation. The ellipsis begins with a space, has three periods with spaces between each, and then ends with a space.

Original quotation: "The Great Wall is something that can be seen from space. When we reach a time when advertisements can be seen from space, we have probably gone too far."

Quotation with words omitted in middle of sentence: Frank Donelson, author of *Signs in Space*, remarks, "The Great Wall…can be seen from space. When we reach a time when advertisements can be seen from space, we have probably gone too far" (178).

If you omit words at the end of a quotation, and that is also the end of your sentence, use an ellipsis plus a period with no space before the ellipsis or after the period.

Original quotation: "The Great Wall is something that can be seen from space. When we reach a time when advertisements can be seen from space, we have probably gone too far with our advertising and signage."

Quotation with words omitted at end of sentence: Frank Donelson, author of *Signs in Space*, remarks, "The Great Wall is something that can be seen from space. When we reach a time when advertisements can be seen from space, we have probably gone too far…." (178).

Citing Online Sources

In the MLA documentation style, online or electronic sources have their own formatting guidelines because these types of sources rarely give specific page numbers.

For better flow and easier understanding, include the name(s) of the person/people (e.g., author(s), editor(s), director(s), performer(s)) responsible for creating your source in the text, rather than in the in-text citation. For instance, the following is the recommended way to begin an in-text citation for an online source:

> Roger Ebert says that Shyamalan "plays the audience like a piano" in the film *Signs* (par. 8).

If the author or creator of the website uses paragraph or page numbers, numbered sections (sec., secs.), or chapters (ch., chs.), use these numbers in the parenthetical citation. If no numbering is used, do not use or add numbers to the paragraphs, pages, or parenthetical citation.

> When website does not number paragraphs: In his review of the film *Signs*, Roger Ebert says that Shyamalan "does what Hitchcock said he wanted to do, and plays the audience like a piano."

> When website numbers paragraphs: In his review of the film *Signs*, Roger Ebert says that Shyamalan "does what Hitchcock said he wanted to do, and plays the audience like a piano" (par. 8).

The Works Cited and Full Citations

Please note that not every single genre or type of citation is included in this section. We have included the most commonly cited sources found in student writing.

General formatting guidelines for the MLA Works Cited

If you use any material from other sources within a paper, be sure to include a Works Cited list at the end of the paper. Here are some general formatting guidelines to follow when setting up a Works Cited.

- Put the Works Cited at the end of your paper as a separate page.
- Use one-inch margins on all sides, and uniform double spacing throughout. Do not add any extra spaces between entries or after the title.
- Page numbers preceded by your last name should continue into your Works Cited from the body of your paper.
- Center the title, Works Cited, at the top of the page, using no underlining, quotation marks, italics, bolding, or other special type or font.
- Place the first line of each entry flush left with the margin. Indent any additional lines of the entry one-half inch (or one tab).
- Alphabetize the Works Cited using the first letter of the last name of the first author listed in each citation. If the cited source does not have an author, alphabetize by using the first word of the source title, not including articles, such as a, an, or the.

- Format your individual Works Cited entries using MLA 8's Core Elements. The most recent edition of the MLA style guide no longer distinguishes between citation formats for digital or print sources. Instead, in an effort to streamline the citation process, MLA 8 relies on a set of nine elements common to most source types. Each element is followed by the punctuation mark shown below, and the last element should be followed by a period. Author. Title of Source. Title of Container, Other Contributors, Version, Number, Publisher, Publication Date, Location. Though MLA 8 makes no distinction between print and digital source types, it is still quite useful to see how the new core elements work with different types of sources. Therefore, the examples that follow are separated into print and digital sections. Furthermore, in these examples, you'll notice that only the elements available for the sample citation are listed in the example Works Cited entry. To clarify, prior to MLA 8, you would include n. pag. if no page numbers were available for your source and n.d. if you didn't have a publication date. That is no longer the case. If a given element is not relevant to the type of source you're citing (e.g. page numbers on a web page), then simply omit it from your Works Cited entry. If you are working with a source type that contains page numbers and our example of that source type does not include them, you should still include them in your Works Cited, since they are relevant to your particular source. MLA 8 recognizes that not all sources have all of the core elements, and even two of the same type sources may not have all of the same core elements. As noted above, if a source is missing any of the core elements, simply omit them from your Works Cited entry.

The sample Works Cited entries on the following pages begin with a simple single-author book entry, containing the Author, Title of Source, Publisher, and Publication Date elements, and build from there. As the source types listed here require additional elements, those elements, their uses, and their functions will be discussed in more detail.

Print Sources

1. Book with one author
When including a source on the Works Cited, be sure to note in the citation which pages you are referencing.

Author. *Title of Source.* Publisher, Publication Date.

Martin, Anna. *Signs.* Dreamspinner, 2015.

Helpful Hint

Omit business words like *Company (Co.), Corporation (Corp.),* and *Limited (Ltd.)* in the *Publisher* element of your Works Cited. For academic publications, replace *University* with *U* and *Press* with *P.* Otherwise, list the full publisher's name. If your source is associated with more than one publisher, separate the publishers' names with a forward slash (*/*).

2. Books with two or more authors

If your source has two authors, format the first author listed with the last name first, and the first name last. Follow this with a comma and the word and, then add the second author's first then last name.

Last Name, First Name (first author), and First Name Last Name (second author). *Title of Source*. Publisher, Publication Date.

Childs, Mark, and Ellen D. Babcock. *The Zeon Files: Art and Design of Historic Route 66 Signs*. U of New Mexico P, 2016.

If a book has three or more authors, you should list only the first author followed by a comma and et al. in place of the rest of the authors' names.

Author, et al. *Title of Source*. Publisher, Publication Date.

Wysocki, Anne Frances, et al. *Writing New Media: Theory and Applications for Expanding the Teaching of Composition*. Utah State UP, 2004.

3. Two books by the same author(s)

Use the author's or authors' full name(s) in only the first entry, then use three hyphens in place of the name(s) in all consecutive entries. The hyphens stand for exactly the same name(s) in the preceding entry, but remember to add any necessary qualifiers (editor, translator, etc.) by following the hyphens with a comma and the term describing that person's role. If the author name changes in any way (for example, an author might add a middle initial) or is combined with different authors than in the first entry listed, format the entry as you normally would, not using any hyphens. Alphabetize all sources by the same author by their titles.

Borroff, Marie. *Language and the Poet: Verbal Artistry in Frost*, Stevens, and Moore. U of Chicago P, 1979.

---, editor. *Wallace Stevens: A Collection of Critical Essays*. Prentice-Hall, 1963.

Both of the above examples include the Version element of MLA 8. If your source indicates that it is one version of a work released in multiple forms, include reference to the version you consulted in your citation. The most common versions you will likely encounter are editions; however, works in other media, especially music and film, often offer different versions of a given album or DVD.

4. Anthology or collection

When citing a complete anthology or collection, which might contain multiple essays, articles, stories, poems, and/or other types of works, the editor(s) fill the author element for your entry. The term author spans a range of possibilities in MLA 8. The individual who fits the author role for your Works Cited entry might actually be an editor, translator, performer, creator, adapter, director, illustrator, or narrator. The key question to ask yourself when trying to determine who to list as your author is: "Who or what aspect in this work am I focusing on in my discussion?" You will only list an editor as your author if you are focusing specifically on the content written or chosen by that editor for the source you've referenced. Otherwise, you should list the individual author of the piece within the edited collection, placing the editor(s), instead, in the role of *Other Contributors*. No matter what role the person or people who fill your author element played in the production of your source, you should follow the same formatting guidelines for one, two, and three or more authors.

Author, editor(s). *Title of Source*. Publisher, Publication Date.

Iyengar, Sujata, and Allison Kellar Lenhardt, editors. *Health*. Fountainhead P, 2013.

5. Work within an anthology, collection, or reference book

When your source forms only a part of a larger whole, you need to provide both the *Title of Container* and *Location* elements in your Works Cited entry to ensure your readers can easily access the information. Additionally, these types of sources often have *Other Contributors* such as editors, translators, and illustrators to name just a few.

Just like it sounds, the container is what holds the smaller source you're actually citing. In addition to an anthology, collection, or reference book, a container can also be a magazine, newspaper, journal, or even a television series. Anytime your source is part of a larger whole, you should be sure to include the title of that larger whole, usually italicized.

Specifying your source's location is one of the only elements of MLA 8 affected by publication medium. Use *p.* to indicate a single page and *pp.* to indicate a range of pages for print sources. When citing websites, you will include the entire web address in the location element.

Like the *Author* element, *Other Contributors* encompass a wide range of possible roles. This element allows you to note individuals who were instrumental in your source's production, even if they weren't solely responsible for its creation. Other contributors roles are indicated using a description, such as performance by, translated by, or directed by. If such a description does not fit the type of contributor you need to cite for your source, use a noun or noun phrase followed by a comma. For example: general editor, John Smith.

Author. "Title of Source." *Title of Container*, Other Contributors, Publisher, Publication Date, Location.

Chandaria, Kartik. "Weather and Language Lessons." *Health*, edited by Sujata Iyengar and Allison K. Lenhardt, Fountainhead P, 2013, pp. 141-44.

6. Work in an anthology that is reprinted from another original publication source

If a text originally appeared in another journal or book before it was reprinted in an anthology, you can include the original publication information followed by the phrase "Rpt. in" and then the new publication information.

Author. "Title of Source." *Title of Container*, Publisher, Publication Date, Location. Rpt. in Author, editor(s). *Title of Source*, Publisher, Publication Date.

Marro, Victora. "The Genres of Chi Omega: An Activity Analysis." *Stylus: A Journal of First-Year Writing*, vol. 3, no. 1, 2012, pp. 25-32. Rpt. in Wardle, Elizabeth and Doug Downs, editors. *Writing about Writing: A College Reader*, Bedford/St. Martin's, 2014, pp. 302-13.

Fishman, Andrea R. "Becoming Literate: A Lesson from the Amish." *The Right to Literacy*, edited by Andrea Lunsford et al., MLA, 1990, pp. 29-38. Rpt. in Bryan Matthew, et al., editors. *UCF Writes*, Fountainhead P, 2016, pp. 6-15.

7. Article in a periodical

Sources such as journals, magazines, and newspapers are all periodicals. When citing a selection from one of these sources, you will need to indicate the periodical's volume (*vol.*) and number (*no.*) in the *Number* element. As with all of MLA 8's core elements, if your particular periodical does not contain all of the information for *Number*, simply include what it does offer. Likewise, if your periodical does not indicate a number of any kind, simply leave out that element.

Author. "Title of Source." *Title of Container,* Number, Publication Date, Location.

Holbrook, Teri. "An Ability Traitor at Work: A Treasonous Call to Subvert Writing from Within." *Qualitative Inquiry,* vol. 16, no. 3, 2010, pp. 171-83.

8. Review

If your review is titled, list the title in the *Title of Source* element, treating the review as any other selection from within a larger container. If your review is not titled, however, then your title will be the words, *Review of*, followed by the title of the work reviewed, then the word, *by*, and the reviewed work's author.

Author. "Title of Source." *Title of Container,* Publication Date, Location.

Ebert, Roger. "A Monosyllabic Superhero Who Wouldn't Pass the Turing Test." *Chicago Sun-Times*, 29 Apr. 2009, p. E4.

Stephenson, M.S. Review of *Apocalyptic Sentimentalism: Love and Fear in U.S. Antebellum Literature*, by Kevin Pelletier. Choice, May 2015, p. 1500.

9. Religious works

Religious works do not often reference an author; therefore, your Works Cited entry will most likely begin with the title of the work. Be sure to pay close attention to the particular version of the text you're referencing, as this will sometimes be the only means of direction by which your reader can locate your original source material.

Title of Source. Version, Publisher, Publication Date.

The Bible. Authorized King James Version, Oxford UP, 1998.

Online Sources

Helpful Hint

Although MLA 8 recommends including URLs for online sources in the Location element of your Works Cited entries, defer to your instructor's preference about this. When including the URL, copy it fully from your browser, omitting only the *http://* or *https://*. If possible, provide a stable URL (permalink) or Digital Object Identifier (DOI) as a more reliable alternative to the browser address.

1. Website

Many websites are associated with a company or organization, but the key publisher's name can often be found either at the bottom of the site's home page or, if one is offered, on the site's "About" page. If the website you're citing includes an author or creator, then include it in your Works Cited entry. If not, begin your entry with the site title.

Title of Source, Publisher, Publication Date, Location.

Everyday Health. Everyday Health Media, 2016, www.everydayhealth.com.

2. Course of department website

Author's/Instructor's Name. *Title of Course,* Name of Department, Name of Institution, Date of posting. Web. Date of access.

Wardle, Elizabeth. *ENC5705: Theory & Practice in Composition.* Department of Writing and Rhetoric, University of Central Florida, 2013. Web. 15 Jan. 2016.

3. Article or item on a website (including blogs, wikis, vlogs, and online audio and video streaming services)

Author. "Title of Source." *Title of Container,* Publisher, Publication Date, Location.

Note: If there is no author given, begin the citation with the article title.

George, Nancie. "6 Unusual Signs of Dehydration." *Everyday Health,* Everyday Health Media, 5 May 2016, www.everydayhealth.com/news/unusual-signs-of-dehydration/.

Chan, Evans. "Postmodernism and Hong Kong Cinema." *Postmodern Culture,* vol. 10, no. 3, May 2000. Project Muse, doi:10.1353/pmc.2000.0021.

Helpful Hint

Avoid citing URLs produced by shortening services like TinyURL and bit.ly. These URLs may stop working if the service that produced them disappears.

4. Online journal article

Author. "Title of Source." *Title of Container,* Number, Publication Date, Location.

Austen, Veronica. "Writing Spaces: Performances of the Word." *Kairos,* vol. 8, no. 1, 2003, kairos.technorhetoric.net/8.1/binder2.html?coverweb/austen/austen.html.

5. Article from an online database or service, such as General OneFile or LexisNexis

When you access a source through a database or service, such as JSTOR, Google Books, or even Netflix, you are using a source located through "nested" containers. A journal article on a database is held in the smaller container, the journal, and that journal is held by the larger container, the database. In your Works Cited, you should attempt to account for all the containers enclosing your source. To do this, you will simply add the core elements, 3-9 (*Title of Container* through *Location*), omitting irrelevant or unavailable elements, to the end of the entry until all additional containers are accounted for.

Author. "Title of Source." *Title of Container,* Number, Publication Date, Location. *Title of Container,* Location.

Pavienko, Sonia, and Christina Bojan. "Exercising Democracy in Universities: The Gap between Words and Actions." *AUDEM: The International Journal of Higher Education and Democracy,* vol. 4, 2015, pp. 26–37. *Project Muse,* muse.jhu.edu/article/557647.

In the above example, the first container is the journal, *AUDEM*, and the second is the journal database, Project Muse. Since the location is the last element in the first container, it is followed by a period. You'll note that, especially in the second container, many of the core elements are missing. Indeed, only the title and location are available for the second container, and this is fine. As noted previously, simply omit those elements that are irrelevant to the container you're working with.

6. Comments on blogs, videos, or social media, etc.

You may occasionally need to cite untitled web sources, such as comments on a blog, images, or Tweets. There are a few ways to approach this. If your source is untitled, provide a description, neither italicized nor in quotation marks, to fill the title element. Use sentence rather than title capitalization.

Title of Source. *Title of Container,* Location.

Kitten wearing a sweater. *Google Images,* img.buzzfeed.com/buzzfeed-static/static/2014-11/4/14/ enhanced/webdr06/enhanced-24665-1415129188-3.jpg.

Your description might contain the title of another work if it's commenting on or responding to that work. This will be the case if you wish to cite comments on a blog post or other such interactions as sources. Note also that MLA 8 allows for the inclusion of usernames or "handles" in the *Author* element.

Author. "Title of Source." *Title of Container*, Publication Date, Location.

> Jeane. Comment on "The Reading Brain: Differences between Digital and Print." *So Many Books,* 25 Apr. 2013, 10:30 p.m., somanybooksblog.com/2013/04/25/the-reading-brain-differences-between-digital-and-print#comment-83030.

Short, untitled messages, such as Tweets, are cited by typing the full text of the message, without any changes, in the *Title of Source* element, enclosed in quotation marks.

Author. "Title of Source." *Title of Container,* Publication Date, Location.

> @persiankiwi. "We have report of large street battles in east & west of Tehran now - #Iranelection." *Twitter*, 23 June 2009, 11:15 a.m., twitter.com/persiankiwi/status/2298106072.

To document an email, use the subject line as the title, and enclose it in quotation marks.

Author. "Title of Source." Other Contributors, Publication Date.

> Boyle, Anthony T. "Re: Utopia." Received by Daniel J. Cahill, 21 June 1997.

7. YouTube video
   Author's Name or Poster's Username. "Title of Video." Publisher, Date of posting, Date retrieved.

> Babak, Larissa. "A Pedagogy of Multiliteracies: Designing Social Futures." YouTube, 6 April 2015. Web. 14 Jan. 2016.

8. Tweet
   Author's Name (Poster's Username). "Text of tweet." Date of posting, Time of posting. Tweet.

> WAC @ UCF (@ucfwac). "Check out the #Writing Assignments in the Disciplines our #WAC Fellows made for their courses wac.cah.ucf.edu/node/151 pic.twitter.com/aGd95qRiHV." 29 Aug. 2015, 7:33 a.m. Tweet.

9. eBook (from a database) with a single author or editor
   Author's Name. *Title of Source*, Publisher, Year of publication. Name of database, Date accessed.

> Jayaprakash, Sajitha. *Technical Writing,* Himalaya Pub. House, 2008. UCF Online General Collection, 16 Jan. 2015.

10. eBook on a Kindle, Nook, iPad, or other reader
    Author's Name. *Title of Source.* Publisher, Year of publication. File type used by eBook reader.

> Shakespeare, William. *Romeo and Juliet*, Feedbooks, 1597. ePub.

11. PDF file (web document)
   Author's Name. *Title of Source.* Publisher, Year of publication. PDF file.

Adobe Systems Incorporated. *Creating Accessible Adobe PDF Files: A Guide for Document Authors,* Adobe, 2004. PDF file.

12. Microsoft Word file
   Author's Name. "Title of Source." Year of publication. *Microsoft* Word file.

Pompos, Melissa. "Reading Journal Expectations." 2016. *Microsoft Word file.*

Other Common Sources

1. Television or radio program

Media sources require special consideration when it comes to the *Author* and *Other Contributors* elements. Remember that the deciding factor in this situation is the aspect of the source you're focusing on. If you're discussing Matthew Gray Gubler's performance as Dr. Spencer Reid in *Criminal Minds*, you would list "Gubler, Matthew Gray, performer." in the *Author* element (as in the first example), but if you're discussing the same show as a part of Jeff Davis's body of creative work, you would cite "Davis, Jeff, creator." as your author (as in the second example). If you're examining the show or an episode with no particular focus on a performer or other contributor, skip the author element and begin your entry with the episode or show title (as in the last example). Note also how location and publication information changes in each example as they move from a show watched on television, to the same show viewed via Netflix, and lastly, that show seen on DVD.

Gubler, Matthew Gray, performer. "Mr. Scratch." *Criminal Minds,* directed by Matthew Gray Gubler, season 10, episode 21, FOX, 22 Apr. 2015.

Davis, Jeff, creator. "Mr. Scratch." *Criminal Minds,* directed by Matthew Gray Gubler, season 10, episode 21, FOX, 22 Apr. 2015. *Netflix,* www.netflix.com/watch/80066884?trackId=14170289&tctx=0%2C20%2C952df56e-847a-4278-a591-d2417455114f-109029147.

"Mr. Scratch." *Criminal Minds: Season 10,* created by Jeff Davis, directed by Matthew Gray Gubler, episode 21, Paramount, 2015, disc. 6.

2. Sound recording

Artist. "Title of Source." *Title of Container,* Publisher, Publication Date.

Five Man Electrical Band. "Signs." *Good-byes and Butterflies.* Lionel Records, 1970.

Tesla. "Signs (Live)." 10 Live!, Sanctuary Records, 3 Jun 2014. Prime Music, Amazon, www.amazon.com/gp/product/B00K9FVUDM?ie=UTF8&keywords=tesla%20signs&qid=1463621153&ref_=sr_1_1&s=dmusic&sr=1-1.

3. Film

Films are handled very similarly to television shows. Your author and other contributors should be chosen based on the aspect of the film you examine in your research. If you do not focus on a particular individual, begin your entry with the film title.

Title of Source. Other Contributors, Publisher, Publication Date.

Signs. Directed by M. Night Shyamalan, performance by Mel Gibson, Touchstone, 2002.

4. Advertisement

Since advertisements aren't typically titled, follow the guidelines for providing a description in place of a title.

Name of product, company, or institution. Advertisement. Publisher date of publication. Medium of publication.

SunChips advertisement. *Newsweek,* 15 Jan. 2010, p. 33.

SunChips advertisement. NBC, 15 Jan. 2010, 10:32 p.m.

Note the difference in how the citations for print and television advertisements are formatted.

5. Painting, sculpture, or photograph

When viewing a physical object, such as a piece of art, in person, the "publisher" of the piece is the museum or gallery, etc. displaying the object. The location in this case is quite literal: Cite the city in which you viewed the piece.

If providing the original date of creation for your source will give your reader more context for your project, place the date(s) immediately following the work's title and follow it with a period.

Author. *Title of Source.* Date of Original Publication. Publisher, Location.

da Vinci, Leonardo. *Mona Lisa.* 1503-6, Louvre, Paris.

If you viewed an object, image, or piece of art online, again, the entity making the piece available to the public fills the *Publisher* element, but you will also include both the physical and online locations of the piece.

van Gogh, Vincent. *Cypresses. European Paintings,* The Metropolitan Museum of Art, New York, www.metmuseum.org/art/collection/search/437980.

6. Interview

Author. Title of source. Other contributors, Publication Date.

Elbow, Peter. Personal interview, interviewed by John Smith, 1 Jan. 2009.

7. Lecture, speech, address, or reading

In certain circumstances, it may be appropriate to include a descriptive term in your Works Cited entry to indicate for your reader the type of source you're citing. Format your citation as usual, following the final element with a period, and then add the descriptive term followed by a period at the end.

Author. "Title of Source." Publisher, Publication Date, Location. Description.

Stephens, Liberty. "The Signs of the Times." MLA Annual Convention, 28 Dec. 2009, Hilton Down

Sample Works Cited Using MLA

Following is an example of how a completed Works Cited would look at the end of your paper.

Your Last Name 14

Works Cited

Davis, Jeff, creator. "Mr. Scratch." *Criminal Minds,* directed by Matthew Gray Gubler, season 10, episode 21, FOX, 22 Apr. 2015. *Netflix,* www.netflix.com/watch/80066884?trackId=14170289&tctx=0%2C20%2C952df56e-847a-4278-a591-d2417455114f-109029147.

Five Man Electrical Band. "Signs." *Good-byes and Butterflies,* Lionel Records, 1970.

Signs. Directed by M. Night Shyamalan, performance by Mel Gibson, Touchstone, 2002.

Stephens, Liberty. "The Signs of the Times." MLA Annual Convention, 28 Dec. 2009, Hilton Downtown, New York. Address.

Figure 3-1: Completed Works Cited page

Other MLA Formatting Concerns

In addition to including both in-text citations and a Works Cited in your paper, you need to follow these formatting rules when writing in MLA style (See Figure 3-2):

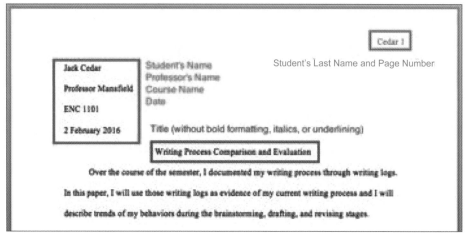

Figure 3-2: Sample paper with header, title, and page numbers

- Use 12 point, Times New Roman font
- Use one-inch (1") margins around all sides of your paper
- Use double-spacing
- Use left alignment for all body text and the heading of your paper
- Center your title and do not apply bold formatting, italics, or underlining
- Add page numbers in the upper right-hand header. The page number should include your last name and the number with nothing in-between.
- Add a *header* to the upper right-left corner of the first page of your paper. The header should include this information in the following order (skipping a line after each part): Your name, your instructor's name, the name of the course, the date.
- When you include illustrations, images, figures, or tables in your paper, you need to add labels, captions, and citations (for content that does not belong to you). *Labels* should appear in two places in your paper: in the body text near the description of the content (e.g., "see Figure 1") and near the content itself ("Figure 1"). *Captions* tell your readers what the title of the content is and/or provide some other kind of explanatory information (e.g. "Figure 1: Menu for January 2016"). If you include content that was authored by someone else, you must include a citation for this content in your Works Cited. You might also want to consider including **alt text** for your visuals. Alt text (alternative text) is text that is inserted into HTML, Microsoft Word documents, or other programs that describes the content of an image. Because some of your readers might not be able to see all the images you include in your paper, they might use screen readers (or other assistive programs) to have that text read to them. If you are interested in adding alt text to your images, search for tutorials such as "Adding Alt Text to Images in Microsoft Word" (The ACCESS Project).

Citing in APA Format

If you write an essay in the social sciences, you will usually be asked to use documentation guidelines created by the American Psychological Association. The Publication Manual of the American Psychological Association, in its sixth edition, provides a full description of the conventions used by this particular community of writers; updates to the APA manual can be found at www.apastyle.org and on the APA Style Blog http://blog.apastyle.org/apastyle/.

Another great citation reference is provided by the Purdue OWL Writing Lab. Their online *APA Formatting and Style Guide* is available at https://owl.english.purdue.edu/owl/resource/560/01/.

Did You Know?

The American Psychological Association was founded in 1892 at Clark University. The APA, now with over 152,000 members, is the primary professional organization for social science scholars in the United States.

In-Text Citations

In APA documentation style, the author's last name (or the title of the work, if no author is listed) and the date of publication must appear in the body text of your paper. The author's name can appear either in the sentence itself or in parentheses following the quotation or paraphrase. The date of publication can appear either in the sentence itself, surrounded by parentheses, or in the parentheses that follow the quotation or paraphrase. The page number(s) always appears in the parentheses following a quotation or close paraphrase.

Your parenthetical citation should give enough information to identify the source that was used for the research material as the same source that is listed in your References list. Where this in-text information is placed depends on how you want to phrase the sentence that is summarized, paraphrased, or quoted. Be sure that the in-text citation guides the reader clearly to the source in the References list, where complete information about the source is given.

The following are some of the most common examples of in-text citations.

1. Author's name and date in reference

    When using a parenthetical reference to a single source by a single author, use this form: (Author's Last name, Year of publication). Note that the period is placed after the parenthetical element ends.

When a teenager sleeps more than 10 hours per night, it is time to question whether she is having significant problems (Jones, 1999).

2. Author's name and date in text

   In APA, you can also give the author's name and date within the sentence, using this form: Author's Full Name (Year of publication)

   Stephanie Jones (1999) describes the signs to look for and when to be concerned.

3. Using a partial quotation in text
   When you cite a specific part of a source, give the page number, using p. (for one page) and pp. (for two or more pages).

   Stephanie Jones (1999) describes the signs parents should look for when concerned about their children: "excessive sleeping, refraining from eating, and lying about simple things" (p. 63).

4. No author given

   When a work has no credited author, use the first two or three words of the work's title or the name that begins the entry in the References list. The title of an article or chapter should be in quotation marks, and the title of a book or periodical should be in italics. Inside the parenthetical citation, place a comma between the title and year.

   In a recent Time article, a list of 30 common signs of teenage trouble cites lack of sleep as the most common sign ("Thirty," 2010).

5. Two to five authors given

   When you use a source that was written by two to five authors, you must use all the names in the citation. For the in-text citation, when a work has two authors, use both names each time the reference occurs in the text. When a work has three to five authors, give all authors the first time the reference occurs in the text, and then, in subsequent citations, use only the surname of the first author followed by et al. (Latin for "and others") and the year for the first citation of the reference in a paragraph.

   The idea that "complexity is a constant in biology" is not an innovative one (Sole & Goodwin, 1997, p. 63).

   The last two authors' names in a string of three to five authors are separated by a comma and an ampersand (e.g., Jones, Smith, Black, & White).

   Most signs in English that the authors encountered on the road had "grammar mistakes, misspellings, or just odd pictures" (Smith, Jones, & Best, 1999, p. 55). The most common mistake was an "incorrect or misplaced apostrophe" (Smith, et al., p. 56).

6. Six or more authors given

   When there are six authors or more of an item to be cited, include only the first author's name followed by et al. (Latin for "and others"). Use this form for the first reference of this text and all references of this text after that. Note: be sure, though, to list all six or more of the authors in your References list.

> In Hong Kong, most signs are in Chinese and English; however, once you are in mainland China, English is rarely found on signs, except in tourist areas (Li, et al., 2007).

7. Authors with the same last names

If your source material includes items by authors who happen to have the same last name, be sure to use each author's initials in all text citations.

> When a teenager sleeps more than 10 hours per night, it is time to question whether she is having significant problems (S. Jones, 1999, p. 63).

> Another sign of trouble can be when you do not see your child for meals (B. Jones, 2003, p. 114).

8. Encyclopedia or dictionary unsigned entry

When you use an encyclopedia or dictionary to look up a word or entry, be sure to include the word or entry title in the parenthetical entry.

> The word thing has more definitions than any other entry in the Oxford English Dictionary ("thing," 2001).

9. Indirect quotation

When you use a quotation of a quotation—that is, a quotation that quotes from another source—use "as cited in" to designate the secondary source.

> Smith has said, "My parents really didn't understand me" (as cited in Jones, 1990, p. 64).

10. Personal communication

Personal communications—private letters, memos, non-archived emails, interviews—are usually considered unrecoverable information and, as such, are not included in the References list. However, you do include them in parenthetical form in the text, giving the initials and surname of the communicator and providing as exact a date as possible.

> A. D. Smith (personal communication, February 2, 2010)

> J. Elbow (personal interview, January 6, 2009)

Using long or block quotations

Long or block quotations have special formatting requirements of their own. If your quotation is prose and longer than 40 words, this is called a **block quotation**. Follow these APA guidelines for block quotations.

- If introducing the block quotation with a sentence, use a colon at the end of the sentence.
- Begin the quotation on a new line.
- Do not use quotation marks to enclose the block quote.
- Indent the quote five spaces from the left margin, and extend the right margin to the end of the line.

- Double space the entire quotation.
- Indent the first line of any additional paragraph.
- Put a period at the end of the quotation, and then add the parenthetical citation.

However, Lansky (1999) states:

> Despite the statement on www.signspotting.com that we don't accept signs with the intention of being funny, people like sending them in. I've opted not to use these as it could encourage people to start mak-ing them, sticking them up in their driveway, and snapping a picture. Plus, funny signs are so much more amusing when the humor is accidental. (p. 72)

Adding or Omitting Words in a Quotation

1. Adding words in a quotation

   Use square brackets ([ ]) to point out words or phrases that are not part of the original text.

   Original quotation:"When we entered the People's Republic of China, we noticed that the signage began dropping English translations" (Donelson, 2001, p. 141).

   Quotation with added word: She said,"When we entered the People's Republic of China, [Dunkirk and I] noticed that the signage began dropping English translations" (Donelson, 2001, p. 141).

   You can also add your own comments inside a quotation by using square brackets. For example, you can add the word sic to a quotation when you know that there is an error.

   Original quotation:"When we entered the People's Repulic of China, we noticed that the signage began dropping English translations" (Donelson, 2001, p. 141).

   Quotation with added comment: She said, "When we entered the People's Repulic [sic] of China, we noticed that the signage began dropping English translations" (Donelson, 2001, p. 141).

2. Omitting words in a quotation

   Use an ellipsis …) to represent words that you delete from a quotation. The ellipsis begins with a space, then has three periods with spaces between them, and then ends with a space.

   Original quotation: "The Great Wall is something that can be seen from space. When we reach a time when advertisements can be seen from space, we have probably gone too far" (Jones, 1993, p. 101).

   Quotation with words omitted in middle of sentence: Frank Jones, author of Signs in Space, remarks, "The Great Wall…can be seen from space. When we reach a time when advertisements can be seen from space, we have probably gone too far" (1993, p. 101).

If you omit words at the end of a quotation, and that is also the end of your sentence, you should use an ellipsis plus a period with no space before the ellipsis or after the period. Only use an ellipsis if words have been omitted.

> Original quotation: "The Great Wall is something that can be seen from space. When we reach a time when advertisements can be seen from space, we have probably gone too far with our advertising and signage" (Jones, 1993, p. 45).

> Quotation with words omitted at end of sentence: Frank Jones, author of Signs in Space, remarks, "The Great Wall is something that can be seen from space. When we reach a time when advertisements can be seen from space, we have probably gone too far . . . ." (1993, p. 45).

Citing Online Sources

In the APA documentation style, online or electronic sources have their own formatting guidelines since these types of sources rarely give specific page numbers.

The APA recommends that you include in the text, rather than in an in- text citation, the name(s) of the person that begins the matching References list entry. If the author or creator of the Web site uses paragraph or page numbers, use these numbers in the parenthetical citation. If no numbering is used, do not use or add numbers to the paragraphs, pages, or parenthetical citation.

When Web site does not number paragraphs

> In his review of the film *Signs*, Roger Ebert says that Shyamalan "does what Hitchcock said he wanted to do, and plays the audience like a piano."

When Web site numbers paragraphs

> In his review of the file *Signs*, Roger Ebert says that Shyamalan "does what Hitchcock said he wanted to do, and plays the audience like a piano" (para. 8).

The References List and Full Citations

Please note that not every single genre or type of citation is included in this section. We have included the most commonly cited sources found in student writing.

General formatting guidelines for the APA References list

If you cite any sources within a paper, be sure to include a References list at the end of the paper. Here are some general formatting guidelines to follow when setting up a References list.

- Put the References list at the end of your paper as a separate page.
- Use one-inch margins on all sides.
- Include any header used for the paper on the References page.
- Center the title **References** at the top of the page, using no underlining, quotation marks, or italics.

- Place the first line of each entry flush left with the margin. Indent any additional lines of the entry one-half inch (or one tab) to form a hanging indent.
- Double space the entries in the References list, not adding any extra spaces between entries.
- Alphabetize the References list. Use the first major word in each entry, not including articles such as *a, an,* or *the,* to determine the alphabetical order. If the cited source does not have an author, alphabetize by using the first word of the title of the source.
- Put author's last name first and then the initial representing the author's first name and the initial for the author's middle name, if given (e.g., Ebert, R.). If a work has more than one author, invert all the authors' names, follow each with a comma, and then continue listing all the authors, putting a comma and ampersand (, &) before the final name (e.g., Ebert, R., & Siskel, G.).
- Arrange two or more works by the same author(s) in the same name order by year of publication.
- Capitalize only the first word in a title and a subtitle unless the title or subtitle includes a proper noun, which would also be capitalized.
- Do not use quotation marks for titles of shorter works, including articles, book chapters, episodes on television or radio, poems, and short stories.
- Italicize the titles of longer works, including album or CD titles, art pieces, books, films, journals, magazines, newspapers, and television shows.
- Give the edition number for works with more than one edition [e.g., *Publication manual of the American Psychological Association* (6th ed.)].
- Include the DOI (digital object identifier), a unique alpha-numeric string assigned by a registration agency that helps identify content and provides a link to the source online. All DOI numbers begin with a *10* and contain a prefix and suffix separated by a slash (for example, 10.11037/0278-6133.27.3.379). The DOI is usually found in the citation detail or on the first page of an electronic journal article near the copyright notice.

Print Sources

1. Books (includes brochures, pamphlets, and graphic novels)

   Author's Last name, Author's Initial of first name. (Year of publication). *Title of book*. Place of publication: Publisher.

   Lansky, D. (2005). Signspotting. Oakland, CA: Lonely Planet.

2. Books with two or more authors
   A comma is used between the author names, even if there are only two authors. First Author's Last name, First author's Initial of first name, & Second author's Last name, Second author's Initial of first name. (year of publication). *Title of book*. Place of publication: Publisher.

Maasik, S., & Soloman, J. (2008). *Signs of life in the USA: Readings on popular culture for writers.* Boston, MA: Bedford/St. Martin's.

3. Two books by the same author
   Be sure the entries are in sequential time order with earliest date first.

Maasik, S., & Soloman, J. (2004). *California dreams and realities: Readings for critical thinkers and writers* (3rd ed.). Boston, MA: Bedford/St. Martin's.

Maasik, S., & Soloman, J. (2008). *Signs of life in the USA: Readings on popular culture for writers.* Boston, MA: Bedford/St. Martin's.

4. Anthology or collection

   Editor's Last name, Editor's Initial of first name. (Ed). (Year of publication). *Title of book.* Place of publication: Publisher.

E. Wardle & D. Downs (Eds.). (2014). *Writing about Writing: A college reader.* Boston: Bedford/St. Martins.

5. Work within an anthology or collection

   Author's Last name, Author's Initial of first name. (Year of publication). Title of work. In Editor's Name(s) (Ed.) *Title of anthology* (page numbers). Place of publication: Publisher.

Marro, V. (2014). The genres of Chi Omega: An activity analysis. In E. Wardle & D. Downs (Eds.). *Writing about Writing: A college reader* (pp. 302-13). Boston: Bedford/St. Martins.

6. Article in a scholarly journal without DOI (digital object identifier)

   Include the issue number if the journal is paginated by issue. If there is not a DOI available and the article was found online, give the URL of the journal home page.

   Author's Last name, Author's Initial of first name. (Year of publication). Title of the article. *Journal Title, volume number* (issue number), pages. URL (if retrieved online).

Holbrook, T. (2010). An ability traitor at work: A treasonous call to subvert writing from within. *Qualitative Inquiry,* 16 (3), 171-183. Retrieved from E-Journals database.

7. Article in a scholarly journal with DOI (digital object identifier)

   Author's Last name, Author's Initial of first name. (Year of publication). Title of the article. *Journal Title, volume number* (issue number), pages. doi:

Franks, L. (2006). The play in language. *Child Signs,* 73(1), 3-17. doi:10.1770/69873629

8. Article in a newspaper
   Use p. or pp. before the page numbers in references of newspapers.

Note: if the newspaper article appears on discontinuous pages, be sure to give all the page numbers, separating them with a comma (e.g., pp. A4, A10, A13- 14).

Author's Last name, Author's Initial of first name. (Year of publication, Month and Date of publication). Title of article. *Newspaper Title*, pp. page numbers.

Genzlinger, N. (2010, April 6). Autism is another thing that families share. *The New York Times*, p. A4.

9. Article in a magazine

Author's Last name, Author's Initial of first name. (Year of publication, Month of publication). Title of article. Magazine Title, volume number (issue number), pages.

Note: only use day if magazine is published on a weekly or bi-weekly basis.

Musico, C. (2009, November). Sign 'em up! CRM Magazine, 13(11), 49.

10. Review

Be sure to identify the type of work being reviewed by noting if it is a book, film, television program, painting, song, or other creative work. If the work is a book, include the author name(s) after the book title, separated by a comma. If the work is a film, song, or other media, be sure to include the year of release after the title of the work, separated by a comma.

Reviewer's Last name, Reviewer's Initial of first name. (Year of publication, Month and Date of Publication). Title of review [Review of the work *Title of work,* by Author's Name]. *Magazine or Journal Title*, volume number (issue number), pp. page numbers. doi number (if available).

Turken, R. (2008, May 5). Life outside of the box. [Review of the film Signs, 2002]. Leisure Times, pp. A12.

11. Article in a reference book

Author's Last name, Author's Initial of first name. (Year of publication). Title of chapter or entry. In A. Editor (Ed). *Title of book* (pp. xx-xx). Location: Publisher.

Jones, A. (2003). Semiotics. In B. Smith, R. Lore, and T. Rex (Eds.). *Encyclopedia of signs* (pp. 199-202). Boston, MA: Rutledge.

12. Religious and classical works

In APA, classical religious works, such as the Bible and the Qur'an, and major classical works that originated in Latin or Greek, are not required to have entries in the References list but should include reference to the text within the sentence in the essay. Note: it is always a good idea to check with your instructor on this type of entry since there can be some variety across instructors and schools.

Online Sources

1. Web site

   The documentation form for a Web site can also be used for online message, blog, or video posts.

   Author's Last name, Author's Initial of first name (if author given). (Year, Month Day). *Title of page* [Description of form]. Retrieved from http://www.xxxx

   United States Post Office (2010). *United States Post Office Services Locator* [search engine]. Retrieved from http:// usps.whitepages.com/post_office

2. Article from a Web site, online newspaper, blog, or wiki (with author given)

   Author's Last name, Author's Initial of first name. (Year, Month Day of publication). Title of article. *Name of Webpage/Journal/Newspaper*. Retrieved from http://www.xxxxxxx

   Ebert, R. (2002, August 2). Signs. *Chicago Sun-Times*. Retrieved from http://rogerebert.suntimes. com/

3. Article from a Web site, online newspaper, blog, or wiki (with no author given)

   Title of article. (Year, Month Day of publication). *Name of Webpage/Journal/ Newspaper*. Retrieved from http://www.xxxxxxx

   China's traditional dress: Qipao. (2001, October). *China Today*. Retrieved from http:// chinatoday.com

4. Online journal article

   The reference for an online journal article is set up the same way as for a print one, including the DOI.

   Author's Last name, Author's Initial of first name. (Year of publication). Title of the article. *Journal Title*, *volume number* (issue number), pages. doi:xxxxxxxxxxx

   Franks, L. (2006). The play in language. *Child Signs*, 73(1), 3-17. doi:10.1770/69873629

   If a DOI is not assigned to content you have retrieved online, use the home page URL for the journal or magazine in the reference (e.g., Retrieved from http:// www.xxxxxx).

   Austen, V. (2003). Writing spaces: Performance of the word. *Kairos*. Retrieved from http:// kairos.com

5. Article from an online service, such as General One- File, LexisNexis, JSTOR, ERIC

   When using APA, it is not necessary to include database information as long as you can include the publishing information required in a normal citation. Note: this is quite different from using MLA documentation, which requires full information about the database.

6. Article in an online reference work
   Author's Last name, Author's Initial of first name. (Year of publication). Title of chapter or entry. In A. Editor (Ed). *Title of book*. Retrieved from http://xxxxxxxxx

   Jones, A. (2003). Semiotics. In B. Smith, R. Lore, and T. Rex (Eds.). *Encyclopedia of signs*. Retrieved from http:// brown.edu/signs

7. YouTube video
   Author's Last name, Author's Initial of first name [Screen name]. (Year of publication, Month day). *Title of video* [video file]. Retrieved from URL.

   Babak, L. (2015, April 6). *A pedagogy of multiliteracies: Designing social futures* [video file]. Retrieved from https://www.youtube.com/watch?v=lMOMf1uNdYk

8. Tweet, Facebook status update, or Google+ post by single author
   Author's Last name, Author's Initial of first name [Screen name]. (Year of publication, Month day). Text of entire tweet [Tweet]. Retrieved from URL.

   WAC @ UCF [@ucfwac]. (2015, August 29). Check out the #Writing Assignments in the Disciplines our #WAC Fellows made for their courses wac.cah.ucf.edu/node/151pic. twitter.com/aGd95qRiHV [Tweet]. Retrieved from https://mobile.twitter.com/ucfwac/status/637634277027500032?p=v

9. eBook
   Author's Last name, Author's Initial of first name. (Year of publication). *Title of eBook* [E-reader version, if applicable]. Retrieved from URL.

   Shakespeare, W. (1597). Romeo and Juliet [eBook]. Retrieved from https://www.goodreads.com/ebooks/download/18135.Romeo_and_Juliet

10. Blog post
    Author's Last name, Author's Initial of first name/ Screen name. (Year of publication, Month day). Title of blog post [Web log]. Retrieved from URL.

    Vie, S. (2015, November 11). Meet Ali Valerio, the first Honors in the Major student in DWR [Web log]. Retrieved from https://compcommunitychronicle.wordpress.com/2015/11/11/meet-ali-valerio-the-first-honors-in-the-major-student-in-dwr/

11. PDF, Online Lecture Notes, and Presentation Slides (e.g., PowerPoint)
    Author's Last name, Author's Initial of first name. (Year of publication). *Title of document* [Type of file]. Retrieved from URL.

    Purdue OWL staff. (n.d.). *APA formatting and style guide* [PowerPoint slides]. Retrieved from https://owl.english.purdue.edu/media/ppt/20081208070939_560.ppt

12. Nonperiodical web document or report
    Author's Last name, Author's Initial of first name. (Year of publication, Month day). *Title of document*. Retrieved from URL.

    Roozen, K., Bryan, M., & Stack, N. (2015). *First-year composition program annual report*. Retrieved from http://writingandrhetoric.cah.ucf.edu/files/report_fyc_14-15.pdf

Other Common Sources

1. Television or radio program (single episode)

   Writer' Last name, Writer's Initial of first name. (Writer), & Director's Last name, Director's Initial of first name. (Director). (Year). Title of episode [Television/ Radio series episode]. In Executive Producer's name (Executive Producer), *Title of show.* Place: Network.

   Bell, J. (Writer), Carter, C. (Creator), & Manners, K. (Director). (2000). Signs and wonders [Television series episode]. In C. Carter (Executive Producer), *The X files*. New York, NY: FOX.

2. Sound recording

   Writer's Last name, Writer's Initial of first name. (Copyright year). Title of song. [Recorded by Artist's name if different from writer]. On *Title of album* [Medium of recording]. Location: Label. (Date of recording if different from song copyright date).

   Emmerson, L. (1970). Signs. [Recorded by Five Man Electrical Band]. On *Good-byes and butterflies* [LP]. New York, NY: Lionel Records.

   Emmerson, L. (1970). Signs. [Recorded by Tesla]. On *Five man acoustical jam* [CD]. New York, NY: Geffen. 1990.

3. Film

   Producer's Last name, Producer's Initial of first name. (Producer), & Director's Last name, Director's Initial of first name. (Director). (Year). *Title of film* [Motion picture]. Country of Origin: Studio.

   Kennedy, K. (Producer), & Shyamalan, M. N. (Director). (2002). *Signs* [film]. USA: Touchstone.

4. Painting, sculpture, or photograph

   Artist's Last name, Artist's Initial of first name. (Year, Month Day). *Title of material.* [Description of material]. Name of collection (if available). Name of Repository, Location.

   Gainsborough, T. (1745). *Conversation in a park.* [Oil painting on canvas]. Louvre, Paris, France.

5. Personal interview

   Unlike MLA documentation, personal interviews and other types of personal communication are not included in APA References lists. Be sure to cite personal communications in the text only.

6. Lecture, speech, address, or reading

   Speaker's Last name, Speaker's Initial of first name. (Year, Month). Title of speech. *Event name.* Lecture conducted from Sponsor, Location.

   Stephens, L. (2009, December). The signs of the times. *MLA annual convention.* Lecture conducted from Hilton Hotel Downtown, New York, NY.

Sample References List using APA

Following is an example of how a completed References list would look at the end of your paper. (See Figure 3-3 below)

Your Last name   14

References

Emmerson, L. (1970). Signs. [Recorded by Five Man Electrical Band]. On *Good-byes and butterflies* [LP]. New York, NY: Lionel Records.

Franks, L. (2006). The play in language. *Child Signs,* 73(1), 3-17.doi: 10.1770/69873629

Kennedy, K. (Producer), & Shyamalan, M. N. (Director). (2002). *Signs* [film]. USA: Touchstone.

Jones, A.(2003). Semiotics. In B. Smith, R. Lore, and T. Rex (Eds.). *Encyclopedia of signs.* Retrieved from http://brown.edu/signs

Lansky, D. (2005). *Signspotting.* Oakland, CA: Lonely Planet.

Stephens, L. (2009, December). The signs of the times, *MLA annual convention.* Lecture conducted from Hilton Hotel Downtown, New York, NY.

Tan, A. (2010). Mother tongue. In R. Bullock, M. D. Goggin, & F. Weinberg (Eds.). *The Norton field guide to writing* (pp. 564-70). New York, NY: Norton

Figure 3-3. Sample References List using APA.

Other APA Formatting Concerns

In addition to including both in-text citations and a References list in your paper, you need to follow these formatting rules when writing in APA style:

- Use 12 point, Times New Roman font
- Use one-inch (1") margins around all sides of your paper
- Use double-spacing
- Use left alignment for all body text and the heading of your paper
- Add a page header or **running head** at the top of every page. On your Title page, include "Running head: TITLE OF PAPER." On all other pages, include a **page header** that states "TITLE OF PAPER." As shown, the title should appear in all capital letters.
- Insert page numbers in the upper right-hand corner of the header.

- Include these four sections in your paper: **Title Page, Abstract, Main Body,** and **References**. Main Body refers to the body text of your paper. References refers to your References list, which appears at the very end of your paper. The Title Page includes the following information: running head, title of paper, author's name, and institutional affiliation. The latter three pieces should appear a few lines below the running head and be centered. Use double spacing throughout. The Abstract includes the page header, the word "Abstract" (centered), and an abstract of approximately 150-250 words.

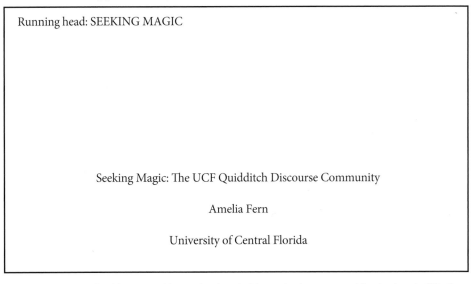

Figure 3-4. Sample Title Page with running head, title, author's name, and institutional affiliation.

Locating Information in Sources for Citations

Sometimes, finding the pieces of information you need to create a citation can be tricky. However, if you know where to look, your job becomes much easier. These are some good places to look for clues about the title, author, publisher, publication date, and other sorts of details you might need to find:

- The title of a book is usually on the front cover, spine, title page, copyright page, and/or Table of Contents. The title might also appear on alternate pages of the header of the body text.
- The title of a journal is usually found on the title page, copyright page, and/or at the top or bottom of the article.
- The title of a website is usually found at the top of the webpage.
- The author of a text is usually listed below the title. In some cases (such as a newspaper article), the author's name might be listed in a byline at the end of the body text.
- The publisher of a book is usually listed on the title page and copyright page, which appear before the Table of Contents (or body text).

UCF WRITES

- The publisher of an article is usually listed on the title page or copyright page near other publication information (such as the volume or issue number). Sometimes, this information appears in the footer of a journal article.
- The publisher and publication date of a website is usually listed at the bottom (or footer) of the webpage, near a © symbol.
- The publication date for books and journals is usually listed on the copyright page. You can find it by looking for the © symbol.

If you would like to see annotated images showing the locations of information for citations, please reference the helpful webpage "Research Foundations: Locate Citation Information" published by Seminole State. It can be accessed at the following URL: http://libguides.seminolestate.edu/researchfoundations/locatecitationinfo.

Works Consulted

APA Style Blog. American Psychological Association, 2016. Web. 15 Jan. 2016.

Elder, Cristyn, Ehren Pflugfelder, and Elizabeth Angeli. "Handout: Quoting Others." *The Purdue OWL.* Purdue U Writing Lab, 11 Nov. 2010. Web. 2 Feb. 2016.

Paiz, Joshua M., Elizabeth Angeli, Jodi Wagner, Elena Lawrick, Kristen Moore, Michael Anderson, Lars Soderlund, Allen Brizee, Russell Keck. "Reference List: Electronic Sources (Web Publications)." *The Purdue OWL.* Purdue U Writing Lab, 27 Mar. 2015. Web. 14 Jan. 2016.

Pellissippi State Community College Libraries. "Citation Guide: MLA & APA: eBook." Pellissippi State Community College Libraries, 2016. Web. 15 Jan. 2016.

Russell, Tony, Allen Brizee, Elizabeth Angeli, Russell Keck, Joshua M. Paiz, Michelle Campbell, Rodrigo Rodríguez-Fuentes, Daniel P. Kenzie, Purdue OWL Staff. "General Format." *The Purdue OWL.* Purdue U Writing Lab, 10 Oct. 2014. Web. 14 Jan. 2016.

---. "MLA Tables, Figures, and Examples." *The Purdue OWL.* Purdue U Writing Lab, 14 Jan. 2016. Web. 2 Feb. 2016.

---. "MLA Works Cited: Electronic Sources (Web Publications)." *The Purdue OWL.* Purdue U Writing Lab, 6 July 2015. Web. 14 Jan. 2016.

---. "MLA Works Cited: Other Common Sources." *The Purdue OWL.* Purdue U Writing Lab, 2 Dec. 2014. Web. 14 Jan. 2016.

"Sic." *Wikipedia*. Wikipedia, 21 Jan. 2016. Web. 2 Feb. 2016.

The Writing Center. "Why We Cite." Online video clip. *Why We Cite – The Writing Center*. The University of North Carolina at Chapel Hill, n.d. Web. 13 Jan. 2016.

Works Cited

The ACCESS Project. "Adding Alt Text to Images in Microsoft Word." Colorado State University, 2010. Web. 2 Feb. 2016.

Cornell University Law School. "Intellectual Property." Legal Information Institute, n.d. Web. 2 Feb. 2016.

Council of Writing Program Administrators (WPA). "Defining and Avoiding Plagiarism: The WPA Statement on Best Practices." Council of Writing Program Administrators, 2003. Web. 14 Jan. 2016.

Driscoll, Dana Lynn, and Allen Brizee. "Quoting, Paraphrasing, and Summarizing." *The Purdue OWL*. Purdue U Writing Lab, 15 Feb. 2013. Web. 14 Jan. 2016.

Russell, Tony, Allen Brizee, Elizabeth Angeli, Russell Keck, Joshua M. Paiz, Michelle Campbell, Rodrigo Rodríguez-Fuentes, Daniel P. Kenzie, Purdue OWL Staff. "MLA In-Text Citations: The Basics." *The Purdue OWL*. Purdue U Writing Lab, 6 Mar. 2014. Web. 14 Jan. 2016.

"Verbs Used in MLA Style Signal Phrases." ISU, n.d. Web. 2 Feb. 2016.

World Intellectual Property Organization (WIPO). "What is Intellectual Property?" WIPO Publication No. 450(E), n.d. Web. PDF file.

CHAPTER 4

Revision

Edited by Adele Richardson

Revision is Part of the Writing Process

In ancient times, the focus of the rhetor was upon the presentation of oral arguments in the form of speeches and students trained to perform in pressured situations before a law court or assembly. Though a speaker might spend time in preparation, most speeches were one-time opportunities. If the words were not well-chosen and well-spoken the first time, there was no second chance to influence an audience.

With modern documents, a composition does not have to be perfect when the words first appear on the page. A document is not truly finished until it is transmitted to an audience, and, even then, important documents are often circulated in draft stages to colleagues for comments before they are presented to an audience.

Many writers claim that revising is the most rewarding step in writing, the time when they have words on a page to work with and can manipulate them to create a composition that communicates effectively. Yet, many students feel that their first drafts should stay exactly the way they've written them because these writings are truest to their feelings and experience. They are sure they have made their point clearly. In reality, early drafts often leave readers scratching their heads and wondering what it was the writer meant to say. To communicate effectively, writers must learn to interact with readers to ensure the clarity of their messages.

Revising versus Editing

At some point during the semester, your instructor will most likely require you to revise one or more of the papers you wrote for class. In many instances, students change some words, add punctuation, and call it revised. But what they really did was edit. There are important differences between these two terms that your instructor will expect you to not only come to understand, but also put into practice.

Different people may use different terminology when discussing revision. Some refer to it as addressing global issues or global concerns; others may talk about it as working on HigherHigher-OrderHigher-Order Concerns. Revising is "big picture" work. It is you putting yourself in the position of the reader and looking at your work from their point of view—and with their expectations. During revision, you look at the paper as a whole and may perform "bigger" operations like reorganizing, rewriting, or even deleting a paragraph or an entire section of the document. You look for ways to improve the quality of your paper. Perhaps you may refine your main claims and the ways you supported them, or reorder the points so your arguments are clearer and more focused. With revision, you're making larger-scale changes.

> When revising, your goal is to re-see or "re-vision" how well you communicated your ideas to your audience.

Editing is different. It may be talked about as paying attention to local issues or local changes; some may call it attending to Lower-Order Concerns. With editing you're reading your paper at a sentence level. Here is where you'll rephrase a sentence, swap out words, or add, remove, or change punctuation. Format concerns such as paragraph indents and font type are also lower-order concerns. Whenever you're making quick, small changes, you're doing simple editing.

Even when the differences between revising and editing are understood, most first-year college students are tempted to edit first because it's faster and easier. This, however, is a mistake. If you edit before you revise, you may make some wonderful changes—and then throw them all away when you have to delete those edited paragraphs. You have, in essence, just wasted a lot of time and effort. So revise first, then edit. For further guidance, the rest of this section includes suggested ideas for performing genuine revision.

Begin Revision by Rereading

The first step of revising is rereading. This step can be simple, if you are reading something written by someone else. When it is your own writing, it becomes infinitely more difficult. After all, you know what you meant to say—you know the research behind the writing and why you chose certain words or phrases. You even know how every sentence is supposed to read—even though you may have left out a word or two or three—and your mind can trick you into seeing the missing words. Unfortunately, the reader does not have your understanding, and communication can break down. You need to learn to read your own work critically, as if it were written by a stranger. One useful aid in this process is to read your work aloud. You can often hear stumbling blocks quicker than you can see them. It's also useful to start early enough so you have some time between rereading and the due date.

The more time you give yourself between readings, the more likely you are to find problems.

At the very minimum, look back over your assignment and class notes and compare everything in your document to the expectations your instructor outlined in the assignment. Below are some ideas to help you with the content of your paper.

Revising for Content

Many times when students are writing and revising, they focus more on word choice and punctuation, but your coursework is most likely evaluated primarily on the content you provided, as well as the effectiveness of your communication. Start with these kinds of global issues when revising.

Main Claims

Ask yourself if the essay is focused on a clear main claim or thesis, and does everything in the paper reflect back on that claim? Look at each paragraph to make sure.

If you have a genuinely focused essay, you should be able to sum up the entire contents in a sentence or two. This is your main claim. If you can't, cut out whatever doesn't reflect back on your thesis. This may mean that you have to narrow down your point(s) so you don't cover too much information. It's better to have a clear, focused, and thoroughly discussed claim than to have a lot of material branching out in different directions for a broad thesis.

Effective Support

Your focused claim or thesis also needs to have reasonable and logical support. You need to be able to show proof of the claims you're making or your credibility lessens. At the bare minimum, explaining why you see things the way you do has to make sense. As you revise, pay attention to the quality and quantity of your research, how you documented your sources (including visuals), and the details of your explanations.

Make sure your support complements your claims. For example, say you're writing a paper on how the school week should be three days instead of five, and for support you quoted several teenagers who said, "Yeah, we don't want to be there anyway." This is not reasonable or logical support at all. There's no evidence or data; only very biased opinion. However, if you cite researchers in the field who've conducted case studies that showed actual proof (tests results, brain scans, etc.) of how giving the brain breaks makes people more effective, then you've incorporated reasonable and logical support that bolsters your claim.

Primary Data

To support your claims, you may be able to use data you collected yourself, providing it is reasonable and logical. Be willing, though, to be critical of your methods and to re-evaluate the type of primary research you did, if necessary. Ask yourself if how you collected data really *shows* proof of your claims. Students sometimes create surveys for proof. Sometimes they're very useful. Most of the time, though, the results are really just saying: "X amount of people think X about X." Make sure you can *show* your proof. This usually means asking strategic questions. If you're making claims about questionable rhetoric on canned food labels, you could take side by side pictures to *show* your readers the evidence, instead of just telling them what you think. The bottom line is: during revision, you may find out you need to re-vision how you collected and worked with data, which sometimes means starting over.

Focus

At times, students lose focus in a paper because they wander away from the requirements of the assignment. Your instructor has certain expectations that are probably in the assignment instructions, so make sure you've created the needed type of document. You may have written a wonderful reflection on your experience in a discourse community. But if the assignment asked you to write a genre analysis, you've missed the mark. So, while you need a clear and narrowed claim and topic sentences throughout, you also need to make sure you're producing what's required. Delete from your paper areas that don't fulfill the requirements. This can sometimes be painful to do, but removing what wasn't asked for will only help your writing.

Topic Sentences

Remember to look at each of your paragraphs. Does each one have a topic sentence that relates to your main claim? Then look at what's in each paragraph. Everything included should have something to do with your topic sentence. This strategy can also help you with making sure your paper (and claim) is focused.

Organization

When revising, take note as well as to how you've organized your essay. It should make sense. Many instructors will give you suggestions on how to organize your essay, but no matter what just use common sense. For example, if you've written something similar to an academic journal article, you don't want to discuss how you collected your data after you discuss your results. Each section should transition smoothly into the next. Jumping around in the text is confusing to your reader. When revising, put yourself in your reader's place and think about whether or not your progression of ideas is appealing and logical.

Visuals

Revising is not just about text; you also need to take a critical look at any visuals (charts, graphs, photos, etc.) you may have used. Do they actually help with the claims you're making? Also look at where you placed a visual in your paper. Are they positioned in the right places and at appropriate sizes? Your visuals should have captions to tell what your reader is looking at. If you borrowed it from someone else, you must also cite it. To not do so is stealing.

Importance of Audience

When you write and revise, don't forget that you are writing to an audience other than yourself. Students sometimes expect that every reader is just like them, with similar experiences, memories, and tastes. It's easy to assume that readers are able to understand more than what's written on the page. But as a result of doing so, there may be large gaps in an essay, with an expectation that the reader will fill in exactly the missing information. Make sure you're supplying the information. Add details and be thorough when you explain your points.

Words and Punctuation

Once you've taken care of the Higher-Order Concerns, you can look over the Lower-Order issues, like word choice and repetition. Make sure your words are direct and concrete. It's your job as the writer to paint as clear an image as possible in your readers' minds. Sometimes students use words that make them sound more "academic." Your instructors want you to play with language and expand your vocabulary, but you have to do more than right-click a word with your mouse and look for a synonym. Make sure all the connotations surrounding the word you picked make sense in the context of your essay. If not, you lose credibility.

Pay attention, as well, to overusing words, phrases, and even ideas. When the same word or phrase keeps showing up in a paragraph, your readers start paying attention to how many times it appears instead of your message. A dead giveaway that you're repeating yourself, too, is when you find yourself typing the phrase, "As I mentioned before." This should be a sign for you to stop and delete.

One of the last issues to look over is punctuation. Make sure you are adhering to the rules of the documentation style required by your instructor. In most first-year writing classes, it will either be MLA (Modern Language Association) or APA (American Psychological Association). Use this handbook and any other resources your instructor suggests to guide your punctuation choices.

Proofread

The final step in the revision process is just like the first step: re-read your work again. Putting as much time between drafts and proofreading as possible is ideal, but at some point the assignment has to be turned in. Just make sure you've looked it over before you do!

Additional Resources

You have a tremendous number of resources here at UCF. Your first go-to place is this handbook. Throughout the pages is not only help with how to revise, but also with using and citing sources, punctuation use, and conducting research, to name a few. It can only benefit you to become familiar with what's here, so skim through the table of contents and the handbook pages to discover what is at your disposal.

Another resource is your instructor. You most likely had some class discussion(s) on how to revise, but if you need additional help, look at your syllabus to find out when and where your instructor's office hours are so you can get some personalized help. At the very minimum, you can find the contact information and email him or her with your questions—just do so according to the instructions they provide. Instructors supply this information specifically to help their students outside of the classroom, so take advantage of the opportunities.

Yet another option is the University Writing Center (UWC) where trained consultants can help you with any stage of the writing process. Most of these consultants were, at one time, in the class you're in now, so they understand challenges you're facing—they may even have completed similar assignments. The UWC is free of charge and you can either make an appointment or simply walk in for help. Check out their website at: http://uwc.cah.ucf.edu/

Editing and Revision Samples

The samples below are from Donna Intintolo, an ENC 1101 student at UCF in the fall of 2015. She was arguing that writing was a form of art. Note the differences between editing and revision. In the editing sample, only words and punctuation are addressed. However, during revision, the student realized the examples she gave needed more substance, so she added content to strengthen her argument.

Original Paragraph:

Another form of social media that entails both studio art as well as writing is Instagram. This social media app allows users to post photos of whatever it is they would like to post, while creating clever captions to describe the image. Not all captions entail words, however, sometimes they only include emojis. The purpose of posting the images, a form of art, is equivalent to posting on Twitter or writing in general. The reward in this case, gaining acceptance and attention, is similar to Twitter with favorites and followers.

Edited Version of Paragraph:

One form of social media that is comprised of both studio art and writing is Instagram. This social media app allows users to post photos of whatever it is they would like to post, while creating clever captions to describe the image. Not all captions entail words, however; sometimes they only include emojis. The purpose of posting the images, a form of art, is equivalent to posting on Twitter or writing in general. The reward in this case, gaining acceptance and attention, is similar to Twitter with favorites and followers.

> Using the word "One" instead of "Another" makes the paragraph sound less like a list.

> Replaced "entails" with "is comprised of" and deleted "as well as"

> Replaced comma with semi-colon

Revised Version of Same Paragraph:

One form of social media that is comprised of both studio art and writing is Instagram. This social media app allows users to post photos of whatever it is they would like to post, while creating clever captions to describe the image. Not all captions entail words, however; sometimes they only include emojis. Like art, the captions are limitless and do not have any restrictions. Users could write one word or a whole novel if they really wanted to, with the purpose of finding the best way possible to describe the photo. Many people look for the most appealing way to caption the photos that would capture the viewers' attention while also conveying their intended message. Posting the images, a form of art, is equivalent to posting on Twitter or writing in general because why people use the app relates to my definition of writing. The reward in this case, gaining acceptance and attention, is similar to Twitter with favorites and followers.

> Changed "Another" to "One"

> Replaced comma with semi-colon

> The comparison that I had between Instagram and writing was very weak and didn't add anything to my argument that writing is art. With the sentences that I added, I think that I made the argument that Instagram is both a form of writing and art. The point needed to be stronger because social media is one of the key types of writing that I focused on and in order to make a compelling argument, my examples need substance and they need to make sense.

> Deleted "The purpose of"

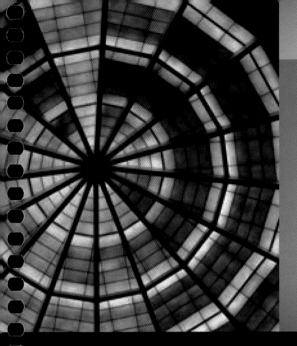

Sentence Construction

Edited by Nathan Holic

Effective writers consider the rhetorical situation in which they're writing. In addition to the other concepts introduced throughout this handbook, these conventions include writing at the basic sentence level, such as grammar, word choice, sentence style, and punctuation. The following sections will provide a brief overview of some important rhetorical choices writers should consider as they construct sentences.

Nouns

A noun is used to identify a person (*teacher, student*), place (*library, garden*), thing (*book, flower*), or idea (*success, joy*). A proper noun names something specific (Knightro, UCF).

Collective nouns indicate a group or unit and are usually viewed as singular.

The **audience** is happy to see signs of life behind the curtain.

I saw my neighbor's **family** drive by with its luggage piled high on top of the car.

If you want to highlight the individuals of a group, then some collective nouns may be treated as plural.

The **audience** are happy that each of their chairs is draped with velvet.

I saw my neighbor's **family** drive by, each of them smiling widely.

Possessive nouns usually signify ownership but can also mark a state of belonging.

Ownership: Jane's book, the student's desk

State of belonging: the book's cover, the desk's legs

Add –'s: if the noun does not end in –s.
  Jane's book, the student's desk

Add –'s: if the noun is singular and ends in –s or an s sound.
  Janis's sign, Giles's desk

Add only an apostrophe if the noun is plural and ends in –s.
the students' desk, the Smiths' house

When you are using proper nouns and want to show that something is jointly owned, mark only the last noun with the appropriate punctuation.

Jane and John's desk, Jane and Giles's desk

When you are using proper nouns and want to show that each individual has ownership, mark each noun with the appropriate punctuation.

Jane's and John's desks, Jane's and Giles's desks

Pronouns

Pronouns are used in place of nouns or noun phrases. When a pronoun substitutes for a specific noun or noun phrase, the word or phrase that has been replaced is known as an antecedent.

In the sentence below, *the daisy* is the noun phrase, and *it* is the pronoun that replaces it.

The daisy is a sign of loyal love; **it** also suggests gentleness and innocence.

There are eight types of pronouns: personal, possessive, reflexive, relative, interrogative, demonstrative, indefinite, and reciprocal.

Personal Pronouns

A personal pronoun indicates a specific person, place, thing, or idea. Personal pronouns can act as subjects or objects, depending on the function of the noun they are replacing. They are also described as singular (one person) or plural (two or more people).

PERSONAL PRONOUNS		
	Subject	**Object**
1st person singular	I	me
2nd person singular	you	you
3rd person singular	he	him
	she	her
	it	it
1st person plural	we	us
2nd person plural	you	you
3rd person plural	they	them

Possessive Pronouns

Possessive pronouns indicate a state of ownership or belonging. They can occur before a noun or after a verb, and they can also be singular or plural.

Possessive pronouns		
	Before a noun	**After a verb**
1st person singular	my	mine
2nd person singular	your	yours
3rd person singular	his	his
	her	hers
	its	its
1st person plural	our	ours
2nd person plural	your	yours
3rd person plural	their	theirs

Reflexive and Intensive Pronouns

Reflexive and intensive pronouns are formed by adding –self or –selves to a personal pronoun. A reflexive pronoun can be an object (direct object, indirect object, or object of a preposition) or a subject complement. Intensive pronouns have the same form as reflexive pronouns and emphasize a noun or another pronoun.

Reflexive/intensive pronouns	
1st person singular	myself
2nd person singular	yourself
3rd person singular	himself
	herself
	itself
1st person plural	ourselves
2nd person plural	yourselves
3rd person plural	themselves

Relative pronouns

Relative pronouns are a type of pronoun that often introduces a dependent or relative clause in a sentence. Relative pronouns include *who, whom, that, which, whose, whoever, whomever, whichever*, and *whatever.*

When floriography was at its peak, more than 400 flower language dictionaries, **which** gave a meaning to each flower, were available.

Use *that* to begin relative clauses that are restrictive and *which* to begin relative clauses that are non-restrictive. When using *which* for a non-restrictive relative clause, be sure to put commas around the entire clause to indicate that it is optional.

Restrictive (essential for sentence meaning):
   The flowers **that** I like are often too expensive to buy.

Non-restrictive (not essential for sentence meaning):
   I planted day lilies, **which** can come in a variety of colors, last spring.

Some relative pronouns are classified as subject and object pronouns. Be sure to use subject-relative pronouns when replacing a subject noun, and object-relative pronouns when replacing an object noun. *Who* is used as the subject and *Whom* is used at the object. *Whose* is a relative pronoun that shows possession.

Relative pronouns			
	Subject	**Object**	**Possessive**
Personal	who	whom	whose
	whoever	whomever	whose
Non-personal	that	that	

Interrogative Pronouns

Interrogative pronouns are used to introduce questions. Some of these can also function as relative pronouns, but when they are used as interrogative pronouns, they trigger the use of a question mark.

Interrogative pronouns: *who, whom, what, which, whose*
   What is the name of the Navy plane that carries the president?
   Who is the pilot today?
   Whom did the president recommend?

Demonstrative Pronouns

Demonstrative pronouns identify, point out, or point to people, places, things, or ideas, usually without naming the noun to which the demonstrative pronoun refers or marks. Demonstrative pronouns can function as noun replacements or as articles/adjectives.

Demonstrative pronouns: *this, that, these, those*

Functioning as article/adjective: **That** book is Paul's.

Functioning as noun: **This** is the correct shelf for the book.

Indefinite Pronouns

Indefinite pronouns refer to unknown or unnamed people, places, things, or ideas. Some are singular, some are plural, and some may be used as either. Indefinite pronouns can function as either noun replacements or as determiners/adjectives.

Some indefinite pronouns: *all, another, anybody, anyone, anything, both, each, each one, either, everybody, everything, few, many, most, neither, none, no one, nothing, one, some, something*

Reciprocal Pronouns

Reciprocal pronouns indicate the individual parts of a plural antecedent noun.

Reciprocal pronouns: *each other, one another*

The pilot and co-pilot were talking to **each other**.

Pronoun/Antecedent Agreement

An antecedent of a pronoun is the word to which the pronoun refers. It usually comes before the pronoun.

When using pronouns to replace or refer to nouns, be sure that the pronoun agrees with its antecedent noun in number, person, case, and gender. Use singular pronouns to refer to singular nouns, and use plural pronouns to refer to plural nouns.

The **pilot** of Air Force One is on-call; **her** phone could ring at any time.

Pilots of Air Force One are on-call; **their** phones could ring at any time.

Subjects

The subject of a sentence includes all words that are part of the phrase (a group of words without a subject-verb component) or clause (a group of words that contain a subject and verb) that is functioning as a noun.

The subject is the part of the sentence about which something is said or described. Pronouns, nouns, noun phrases, and noun clauses can be the subject of a sentence.

Pronouns and nouns as subjects

Single words—pronouns and nouns—can be subjects.

Pronoun: **He** can fly the plane.

Noun: **Sheila** can fly the plane.

Noun phrases and noun clauses as subjects

More complex than single words, noun phrases and noun clauses can also be subjects of sentences.

Noun phrase: **The flight attendant** can fly the plane.

Noun phrase: **The substitute flight attendant who is training to be a pilot** can fly the plane.

Noun clause: **That she can fly the plane** is lucky.

A complete subject that is made up of a noun phrase includes all pre- modifiers and post-modifiers of the head or main noun. Note that pilot is the head—also known as the simple subject—of the following noun phrase, but that the entire noun phrase is the complete subject of the sentence.

The **flight attendant who dropped the soft drinks** left a mess on the floor.

Other parts of speech as subjects

When they are functioning like a noun, other parts of speech, such as verb infinitives (*to + base verb*) or gerunds (*-ing verb*), can also be the subject of a sentence. (Please refer to section below on *Verbals* for more information on gerunds and infinitives.)

Verb infinitive phrase: **To fly the plane** is easy.
Gerund phrase: **Flying the plane** is easy.

Delayed subjects

In English, the subject occurs before the verb in most sentences since English has what is called an S-V-O (Subject-Verb-Object) language pattern. Some sentences, though, can have delayed subjects when a placeholder—*it* or *there*—occurs before the verb, and the delayed subject comes after the verb. Note that these placeholders occur with forms of the *to be* verb.

It has been **some time** since the flight attendant went into the cockpit.
There seems to be **some problem** in the cockpit.

The subject is also delayed in questions.

Where is **the river?**
Why are **we** losing altitude?

Verbs

· ·
Main verbs express action or a state of being, and auxiliary verbs (be, have, do) help conjugate main verbs for tense (present, past, future), voice (active, passive), and aspect (perfect, progressive).
· ·

Verbs or verb phrases can sometimes function as other elements in a sentence, such as a subject.

Main verbs

Main verbs can be divided into three different types: linking, transitive, and intransitive.

Linking verbs

Linking verbs link subjects to a noun (or noun phrase) or adjective (or adjective phrase) in the verb phrase or predicate. Sense verbs, such as *smell* or *taste*, and stative verbs (verb that describe a state of being), such as *seem* or *become*, also function as linking verbs. When a noun or adjective follows a linking verb, it is called a subject complement or predicate noun/predicate adjective.

Common linking verbs
Forms of *to be* – is, am, are, was, were, be, been, being
Sense verbs – smell, sound, appear, taste, feel, look
Other stative (state of being) verbs – seem, become, remain, stay, turn, get

Linking verbs (LV) can also connect subjects to prepositional phrases (PP) that are functioning as adverbial complements, giving necessary information to complete the sentence.

Air Force One **is on the ground**.
      LV| PP |

Transitive verbs

Transitive verbs (Vt) describe an action that is directly received by a direct object, which is needed to complete the action and the meaning of the verb. A direct object (DO) answers one of these questions: Whom? What?

When a president **uses** a **Coast Guard plane**, the call sign for the plane is Coast Guard One.

Note in the above sentence that the direct object (*a Coast Guard plane*) receives the action of the transitive verb (*uses*) directly. What does a president use? A Coast Guard plane.

Transitive verbs (Vt) can also trigger the use of an indirect object (IO), which receives the action of the verb in an indirect manner. An indirect object answers one of these questions: To whom? To what? For whom? For what?

Because of her quick thinking during a disaster, the President **gave** the **pilot** a **medal**.
                                                    | Vt | | IO | | DO |

The President also **awarded** a **veteran** a **Purple Heart**.
         | Vt | | IO | | | DO |

Intransitive verbs

Intransitive verbs (Vi) do not need a direct object since the action of an intransitive verb is complete in and of itself.

When she saw the helicopter approaching too close, the pilot **shouted**.
                                                  | Vi |

The soldier **cried** upon **receiving** the **award**.
         | Vi | | Vi | | DO |

Verbals

Verbals are derived from verbs but function as other parts of speech, including nouns and adjectives. Verbals may take objects or modifiers, just as a verb may. The three types of verbals include gerunds, infinitives, and participles.

Gerunds

Gerunds are verbs that end in -ing and function as nouns.

As subject: **Flying** is difficult.

As object: One difficult part of flying is **knowing** about weather.

Infinitives

Infinitives are *to* plus the base form of verbs.

As subject: **To fly** is difficult.

As direct object: When I go on vacation, I want **to swim**.

Participles

Present participles are verb forms that end in –ing, and past participles end in suffixes such as –ed, –en, –d, –n, or –t. Regular verbs take the –ed suffix, and irregular verbs can take a variety of endings. Participles, whether present or past, function as adjectives, and as such, usually appear before or after the noun they are modifying.

Before noun: The **ear-piercing** plane left the hangar early.

Before noun: The **reconstructed** plane left the hangar early.

Voice of a verb

The voice of a verb refers to the relationship the subject has with the verb. If the subject is doing the acting, *active voice* is used. If the subject of the sentence is receiving the action, *passive voice* is used. Use the passive voice according to the rhetorical situation. Often, passive voice is advised against in academic writing; it is, however, frequently used when writing about science and technology, when the direct object should be emphasized, or when the actual subject is anonymous or being hidden.

Active voice

Active voice indicates that the subject is doing something now (present tense), in the past (past tense), or in the future (future tense).

Present: She **pilots** Air Force One for the president and his staff.

Past: She **piloted** Air Force One all last week without a break.

Future: She **will pilot** Air Force One all next week.

Passive voice

Passive voice indicates that the subject is being (present tense), has been (past tense), or will be (future tense) acted upon. Passive voice is marked by the auxiliary *be* plus the past participle form of the verb.

Present: The plane **is named** Air Force One (by the U.S. Government) because it is an Air Force aircraft.

Past: The plane **was named** Air Force One because it is an Air Force aircraft.

Future: The newly commissioned plane **will be called** *The Enterprise.*

Note that the direct object takes subject position, and the actor/subject is placed in a *by* phrase. This by phrase can sometimes be deleted, and the verb is still passive.

Subject/verb agreement

Subjects and verbs need to agree grammatically. This section highlights some of the most common problems writers have in making subjects and verbs agree.

Check for prepositional phrases

A prepositional phrase can come between a subject and its verb and cause confusion.

<u>Each</u> **of the pilots** is ready to fly Air Force One.

In the previous sentence, *each* is the simple subject or head noun, and it is this simple subject that needs to agree with the verb is.

Check for parenthetical statements or interjections

Parenthetical statements or interjections that interrupt the sentence should not be considered when determining subject-verb agreement. These types of interrupters are easy to spot if punctuated correctly with commas.

The **pilot**, in addition to the co-pilot, was unable to fly the plane.

Scott Johnson, though, was able to take control in the cockpit.

Check for indefinite pronouns as subjects

Most indefinite pronouns when used as subjects take singular verbs. See **Section 2** for a list of indefinite pronouns.

Something is wrong with the cockpit door today. Is that a sign of trouble?

Some indefinite pronouns when used as subjects take plural verbs. These include *both, few, many, others,* and *several.*

Both Sally and John are pilots.

Both are pilots.

Some indefinite pronouns when used as subjects can take either singular or plural verbs. These include *all, any, enough, more, most, none,* and *some.* The noun that the indefinite pronoun refers to determines whether the subject is considered singular or plural.

Check for compound subjects

In compound subjects, there will be more than one head or simple subject.

When the compound subject is joined by *and,* use a plural verb form.

> **She and he** are able to fly the plane.
>
> **Sally and John** always leave when the situation gets uncomfortable.
>
> **The pilot and the co-pilot** always leave the controls unattended.

When the compound subject is joined by *or*, use a singular verb form.

> **She** or **he** is able to fly the plane.
>
> **Sally** or **John** leaves when the situation gets uncomfortable.
>
> When **the pilot** or **co-pilot** leaves the controls unattended, a buzzer sounds in the cockpit.

When the indefinite pronouns *every* and *each* are used before compound subjects, look only at the indefinite pronoun and use a singular verb for subject-verb agreement.

> **Every pilot and co-pilot** learns how to land in dangerous situations.

When the correlative conjunctions *either…or/neither…nor* are used to join compound subjects, the verb should agree with the subject that is closest to the verb.

> Singular: **Neither John nor Sally** is here today to fly the plane.
>
> Plural: **Neither John nor the other pilots** are here

Modifiers: Adjectives

> A modifier is a word that adds to or restricts the sense of a head noun or a verb. An adjective modifies nouns while adverbs modify verbs, adjectives, other adverbs, or even entire clauses.

Forms

Adjectives have three forms: base (or positive), comparative, and superlative. The base form is used when describing one thing without comparing it to anything else.

Types

Adjectives usually occur before the noun they modify; however, they can also occur in subject complement position when they follow a linking verb.

Before the noun: When I was cooking spaghetti, I spilled salt, so I was sure to throw it over **my left** shoulder.

Subject complement: The salt was **messy**, but I did not care at that point.

If two or more words function as an adjective before a noun, use hyphens to join the words together.

One of my **well-known** recipes calls for a lot of salt.

If the two or more words come after the verb, do not hyphenate.

One of my salty recipes is **well known**.

Adjectives can be part of larger adjective phrases. When an adjective has a pre-modifier or a post-modifier, these modifiers are part of the adjective phrase. This is important to know because you would never want to separate an adjective from its modifier with a comma or another type of punctuation. Adverbs (such as *very, so, quite, rather, hardly, frequently*) can pre-modify adjectives, and infinitive verbs (such as *to go, to sell, to feel*) and relative clauses (such as *who will go* or *that shares my values*) can post-modify adjectives.

Adjective as single word: The salt was **messy**.

Adjective phrase with pre-modifier: The salt was **very messy**.

Adjective phrase with post-modifier: The salt was **gritty to the touch**.

Adjective phrase with pre-modifier and post-modifier: The salt was **so messy that I had to stop cooking and clean it up**.

Modifiers: Adverbs

Adverbs have three forms: base (or positive), comparative, and superlative.

Forms

The **base form** is used when describing one thing without comparing it to anything else.

The band Sign's cover of an Iron Maiden song pleased the crowd **immensely**.

The **comparative form** of an adverb compares one thing to another and uses the suffix *–er* or the words *more* or *less* to make the comparison. Usually, you will use *more* or *less* for adverbs with three or more syllables. Consult a dictionary if you are not sure.

The bass pounded **more heavily** than in the original song.

The **superlative form** of an adverb compares three or more things and uses the suffix –*est* or the words *most* or *least* to make the comparison. Usually, you will use *most* or *least* for adverbs with three or more syllables. Consult a dictionary if you are not sure.

Out of all the concerts I have seen this year, the audience in Iceland reacted the **most enthusiastically** of all.

Some adverbs have irregular comparative and superlative forms.

We thought their cover of the song was performed **better** than the original.

Types

Adverbs can be single words, but they can also be part of larger adverbial phrases. When they occur inside a larger phrase, they can be pre-modified by other adverbs (such as *quite, rather, very, so*), and they can also be post-modified by a prepositional phrase (such as *for her*).

Single adverb: During their performance, they sing **forcefully**.

Adverb with pre-modifier: During their performance, they sing **quite forcefully**.

Adverb with post-modifier: During their performance, they sing **forcefully to the audience**.

Adverb with pre-modifier and post-modifier: During their performance, they sing **quite forcefully to the audience**.

Functions

Adverb functions include those that modify verbs, adjectives, other adverbs, and entire clauses. An adverb's main function is to describe how, when, where, why, how frequently, and how much.

When (modifying the verb): We **left immediately** for Iceland when we discovered the band Sign was having a free concert.

Where (modifying the verb): I **would like to travel there** for the music and the adventure.

Why (modifying a clause): I **have wanted to see the band because of their music.**

How frequently (modifying an adjective): Seeing the band in concert was **more exciting** than any of us had imagined.

How much (modifying another adverb): I yelled **more frequently** at the concert than at any other I have ever attended.

How (modifying an entire clause): **Seriously, I have never had a better time on a trip**.

Adverbs, in the form of adverbial conjunctions (also called conjunctive adverbs or transitions), can connect two sentences together.

Adverbial conjunction: I wanted to see the band; **however,** I was late for the plane.

Common adverbial conjunctions	
accordingly	nevertheless
certainly	nonetheless
consequently	otherwise
furthermore	similarly
hence	hereafter
however	therefore
indeed	thus
instead	undoubtedly
moreover	

The Simple Sentence

A simple sentence contains a subject and main verb combination. There are two kinds of clauses: independent and dependent.

An independent clause, sometimes called a main clause, can stand alone as a simple, but complete, sentence. A dependent clause—with its own subject and verb—can never stand alone and is never part of a simple sentence.

Check for common errors with the simple sentence

1. Check for overuse.

2. Check for fragments.

3. Check for parallelism.

The Compound Sentence

One way to add variety to writing is to use coordination to join simple sentences together. When one coordinates or combines together two simple sentences (or two independent clauses), a compound sentence is created.

Four options are available to create compound sentences, and the option that is chosen determines the punctuation used.

1. Using a comma + conjunction

Independent clauses can be joined in a variety of acceptable ways, and using a comma plus a coordinating conjunction is one of the most popular.

The conjunctions that you can use to join together two independent clauses can be remembered by using the mnemonic device **FANBOYS,** in which each letter represents one conjunction.

F   A   N   B   O   Y   S

for and nor but or   yet so

F	American Sign Language is difficult for me, **for** I studied Signed English.
A	Some students learn American Sign Language, **and** they also learn Signed English.
N	I cannot use American Sign Language, **nor** can I use Signed English.
B	I learned some signs in school, **but** I want to learn more American Sign Language.
O	Maybe I will attend an American Sign Language class, **or** I will attend a special summer camp to learn this interesting language.
Y	Some students know American Sign Language, **yet** it is difficult for them to communicate in countries other than the United States with deaf students from other cultures.
S	In some colleges, American Sign Language is the only signing method used by the faculty, **so** those students who only use Signed English will be at a disadvantage.

2. Using a semicolon

A semi-colon can be used to connect two independent clauses. When using a semicolon in this way, a writer suggests that the two connected clauses are related in some way.

> Some students learn American Sign Language; they can also learn Signed English.

3. Using a semicolon + adverbial conjunction

Another way to connect two independent clauses is with a semi-colon plus an adverbial conjunction (sometimes called a conjunctive adverb). Note that a comma follows the adverbial conjunction.

> Some students attend a school that requires American Sign Language; **therefore,** knowing Signed English is not enough.

Common adverbial conjunctions:
Addition: moreover, furthermore, likewise, finally, addition- ally, also,incidentally, further, similarly, in addition
Contrast: however, nevertheless, in contrast, on the contrary, nonetheless, otherwise, on the other hand, in comparison, conversely, instead

Common adverbial conjunctions:			
Comparison: similarly, likewise, at the same time, comparatively			
Exemplification: for example, for instance, namely, that is			
Intensification: indeed, in fact, moreover, still, certainly, notably, undoubtedly			
Result: therefore, thus, consequently, as a result, finally, hence, then, accordingly, henceforth, subsequently, undoubtedly, in fact			
Time: meanwhile, then, next, finally, still, now, thereafter			

4. Using a colon

Although not as common as the first three methods of joining two independent clauses together, you can also use a colon if the clause following the colon defines or elaborates the clause before the colon.

Common sentence errors with the compound sentence

1. Use a variety of punctuation, conjunctions, and adverbial conjunctions

Be careful when you decide how to join compound sentences. Combining sentences in the same way each time or in a way that creates an obviously consistent pattern will negatively impact your writing. It is best to use a variety of punctuation, conjunctions, and adverbial conjunctions.

2. Check for comma splices

Mistakenly joining two independent clauses together with only a comma creates one of the most frequent sentence errors that writers make. You can fix a comma splice by using one of the four options given above, i.e., using a comma + adverbial conjunction, semicolon, semicolon + adverbial conjunction, or colon.

Comma splice: Some American students learn Signed English as children, they learn American Sign Language as adults.

OK: Some American students learn Signed English as children, and they learn American Sign Language as adults.

OK: Some American students learn Signed English as children; they then learn American Sign Language as adults.

OK: Some American students learn Signed English as children; then, they learn American Sign Language as adults.

3. Check for run-on or fused sentences

If you fail to join two independent clauses together with the appropriate punctuation, you can create another common sentence problem—the run-on or fused sentence.

Run-on/fused sentence: My third-grade teacher taught us some signs they were Signed English.

OK: My third-grade teacher taught us some signs, yet I don't know many now.

OK: My third-grade teacher taught us some signs; they were Signed English.

The Complex Sentence

Another way to add variety to writing is to use subordination and modification to create complex sentences. A complex sentence consists of a simple sentence (also known as an independent clause) plus one or more dependent clauses.

Dependent clauses, like independent clauses, contain a subject and predicate; however, whereas independent clauses can stand alone, dependent clauses are dependent or subordinate to an independent clause and must be attached to that independent clause to form a complete sentence. One can track most dependent clauses back to their independent counterparts, as in the set of sentences below.

Independent clause: Each letter in our alphabet is a sign.

Independent clause: Each letter in our alphabet gives us information about our language's history and sound system.

Complex sentence:
Because each letter in our alphabet is a sign, it gives us information about our language's history.
| *Dependent Clause* | | | *Independent Clause* |

Note that the dependent clause above includes the subordinator "because" at the beginning of the clause. A dependent clause usually begins with a subordinator—also called a subordinating conjunction—or a relative pronoun. A subordinator or relative pronoun gives information about the relationship between the independent and dependent clause.

Common subordinators
Cause – because, since, as if, why
Concession – although, even though, certainly, though
Condition – if, unless, how, rather than, where, whether
Effect – so that, in order that Place – where
Sequence – after, before, while, until
Time – when, as, until, once

Relative pronouns	
whichever	who
what	whoever
that	whom
whatever	whomever
which	whose

Dependent clauses

Dependent clauses can be nominal (used like nouns), adjectival (used like adjectives), or adverbial (used like adverbs). This means that dependent clauses can be used as subjects, objects, or modifiers. Although it is sometimes difficult to distinguish which type of dependent clause is being used, it is a good idea to learn the different clause types because your choice of punctuation depends on how a clause is being used.

Noun (or nominal) clauses

Dependent noun clauses can function as subjects, direct objects, subject complements, objects of prepositions, or appositives. Since these types of clauses are dependent or subordinate, they are always attached to an independent clause or a critical part of an independent clause. Noun clauses usually begin with a relative pronoun or with one of these subordinators: when, where, how, why or whether. There are two types of noun clauses: nominal relative clauses and appositive clauses.

1. Nominal relative clauses

Nominal relative clauses take the place of a subject, direct object, or an object of a preposition. A good way to see whether you are using a nominal relative clause is to see if you can substitute a pronoun (*it, she, he*) for the clause in question.

> Dependent Clause/Nominal Relative Clause: **What sound a letter makes** is complicated.

2. Appositive clauses

Appositive clauses (nouns or clauses that rename another nearby noun) follow nouns that are general or abstract in nature, such as a theory, reason, fact, or story. The appositive clause begins with *that* and provides more information about the abstract noun.

> Dependent Clause/ Appositive Clause: The alphabet disconnection theory **that letters do not clearly match sounds** is widely known by linguists.

It is important to be able to distinguish these dependent clauses as noun clauses because neither one of these dependent noun clauses requires   a comma. Putting a comma around these clauses to highlight them or separate them in some way from the independent clause is a comma error.

3. Adverbial clauses

Adverbial clauses, or dependent clauses that function as an adverb, begin with a subordinator (sometimes called a subordinating conjunction) and usually give information about cause/reason, concession, condition, effect, place, sequence, and time. The clauses do this by answering the questions *when? where? why? how? how frequently?* and *in what manner*? Adverbial clauses are always dependent or subordinate to the main or independent clause.

> **Because she was caught with the freeway sign in her car**, she was arrested for theft.
> | *Adverbial (Dependent) Clause* |

Notice that the adverbial clause above gives the reason why the woman was arrested, thus giving information about cause.

Adverbial clauses can function like adverbs, moving to various points in a sentence. When an adverbial clause is at the beginning of the sentence, use a comma to separate it off from the main or independent clause.

Because the policeman watched him closely, the driver followed the detour sign.

When an adverbial clause appears in the middle of a sentence, it should be set off by placing commas around the adverbial clause.

The driver, **because the policeman watched him closely,** followed the detour sign.

However, when an adverbial clause appears at the end of a sentence, it usually does not take a comma.

The driver followed the detour sign **because the policeman watched him closely.**

Common sentence errors with the complex sentence

1. Check for fragments

Dependent clauses do not express a complete thought, and they need to be attached to an independent clause to be grammatically complete. Because dependent clauses are clauses, they contain a subject and a full verb, a fact that sometimes leads a writer to use a dependent clause as a complete sentence. When dependent clauses are presented as a full sentence, they are fragments.

Fragment: **Because the highway trooper watched him closely.**
| *Dependent Clause* |

OK: The driver took the detour **because the policeman watched him closely.**
| *Dependent Clause* |

Fragment: **When she saw the tornado.**
| *Dependent Clause* |

OK: **When she saw the tornado,** she took it as a sign to take cover.
| *Dependent Clause* |

2. Check for unnecessary commas

A noun clause can replace a subject, direct object, subject complement, or object of a preposition. When using a noun clause to replace these items, avoid placing an unnecessary comma between the noun clause and the rest of the sentence.

Extra comma: **What I like about Saturdays,** is seeing all the yard sale signs in my neighborhood.

OK: **What I like about Saturdays** is seeing all the yard sale signs in my neighborhood.

3. Check for restrictive or non-restrictive punctuation

Be sure to use the correct punctuation for relative clauses. When they provide essential information, they are restrictive and should not have commas. When relative clauses provide non-essential or extra information, they are non-restrictive and should always be separated from the rest of the sentence with commas.

Extra comma: The protester, **who had the derogatory sign**, was removed.

OK: The protester **who had the derogatory sign** was removed.

In the above example, the relative clause gives necessary information— the reason the protester was removed from the lecture. Therefore, the relative clause is restrictive and does not take commas.

Missing comma: Shyamalan who directed Sixth Sense and Signs has not won an Academy Award.

OK: Shyamalan, who directed Sixth Sense and Signs, has not won an Academy Award.

In the example above, the information that Shyamalan directed the movies *Sixth Sense* and *Signs* is not essential to the main point that he has not won an Academy Award. Thus, the relative clause is non-restrictive and needs to have commas surrounding it.

4. Check for adverbial clause punctuation

When including an adverbial clause in writing, be sure to use the appropriate punctuation. If the clause appears at the beginning of the sentence, use a comma between it and the independent clause. If the adverbial clause appears in the middle of the sentence, surround the clause with commas. And, finally, if the adverbial clause appears at the end of the sentence, do not separate the dependent adverbial clause and the independent clause.

Missing comma: **As I left the movie** I saw a sign advertising next week's feature.
OK: **As I left the movie**, I saw a sign advertising next week's feature.

Extra comma: I saw a sign advertising next week's feature, as I left the movie.
OK: I saw a sign advertising next week's feature **as I left the movie**.

The Compound-Complex Sentence

A compound-complex sentence is made up of two or more simple sentences or independent clauses (this is the compound part) and one or more subordinate or dependent clauses (this is the complex part).

While she waited for a sign from the employees (dependent clause), **other shoppers sneaked into the toy store** (independent clause), and **they were the ones fortunate enough to find the most popular toy for Christmas** (independent clause).

When punctuating a compound-complex sentence, both the rules for compound and complex sentences are used. For instance, in the above sentence, the dependent adverbial clause appears at the beginning of the sentence; thus, it needs a comma between it and the independent clause. In addition, the combination of a comma and coordinating conjunction is used to join together the two independent clauses.

Common sentence errors with the compound-complex sentence

Pay attention to the common sentence errors listed below for both compound and complex sentences, and you will be successful in punctuating a compound-complex sentence.

1. Check for run-on or fused sentences

Run-on/fused sentence: Students who use both American Sign Language and Signed English understand that some of the signs are the same and this makes it easier for them to learn both.

OK: **Students who use both American Sign Language and Signed English understand that some of the signs are the same, and this makes it easier for them to learn both.**

2. Check for comma splices

Comma splice: Students who use both American Sign Language and Signed English understand that some of the signs are the same, this makes it easier for them to learn both.

OK: **Students who use both American Sign Language and Signed English understand that some of the signs are the same, and this makes it easier for them to learn both.**

3. Check for fragments

Fragment: Students who use both American Sign Language and Signed English understand that some of the signs.

OK: **Students who use both American Sign Language and Signed   English understand that some of the signs are the same, and this makes it easier for them to learn both.**

Appropriate Word Choice

1. Check for exactness and clarity: Be precise

Make every word and phrase count by making your point in the fewest possible words.

Wordy: In point of fact, in language, a code is a sign or rule that allows you to change a piece of information into another sign, form, or representation, and this new sign, form, or representation does not necessarily have to be of the same system.

Concise: **A code is a sign that changes information into another sign, sometimes not in the same system.**

2. Use specific, concrete words

Student writers often are asked to give their opinions about literature, films, or music. Using vague descriptors such as *good, bad, great, best, greatest,* and *worst* weakens writing. Make descriptions stronger by using specific, concrete words.

Vague: *The Old Man and the Sea* is the best novel.

Specific: **In *The Old Man and the Sea*, Ernest Hemingway depicts the accurate and heart-wrenching life of a fisherman.**

Here is a list of some examples of concrete words:

Using specific, concrete words	
Instead of this...	**Try this...**
blue	azure, cobalt, navy, sea blue, turquoise
car	Ford Escort, Toyota Camry, Volkswagen Beetle
friend	school acquaintance, close friend, movie pal
house	home, abode, igloo, apartment, student dormitories
hungry	famished, ravenous, starving
piece of literature	short story, poem, novel, play
river	Danube, Mississippi, Nile
the city	Austin, Los Angeles, Nashville, New York

3. Delete empty words and phrases

It is not the number of words you use, but the exactness of the words that demonstrates writing maturity. Using empty phrases or expletives, such as *there/it + be*, may be grammatically correct, but you can be more concise by just dropping them.

Wordy: There were only three sailors on *The Enterprise* who knew Morse code.

Concise: **Only three sailors on *The Enterprise* knew Morse code.**

If your instructor assigns a first-person essay, be sure that you do not overuse the empty phrases that can sometimes go along with this type of writing. Some instructors call these empty phrases "weasel words" because they can make your writing sound non-authoritative. By dropping these empty phrases or weasel words, you can present your views with more authority.

Wordy: In my opinion, I think that learning Morse code is difficult.

Concise: Learning Morse code is difficult.

Weasel Words
In my opinion
It is my opinion (that) It is true (that)
To my knowledge
I am sure (that)
I believe (that) I know (that) I think (that)

4. Replace wordy prepositional phrases with more concise adverbs

Wordy descriptions sometimes fill up a lot of space but do not say anything important or necessary. This type of wordiness usually includes unnecessary prepositional phrases that can be deleted without changing any real meaning.

Wordy: In this day and age in the event that a boat has trouble in the water, semaphores or Morse code can be used to signal for help.

Concise: **When in trouble, boaters can use Morse code to signal for help.**

Using adverbs for conciseness	
Replace these prepositional phrases	**with these adverbs**
at all times	always
at that point in time	then
at the present time	now, today
at this moment	now, today
beyond a shadow of a doubt	certainly, surely
due to the fact that	because
for the purpose of	for
in order to	to
in point of fact	undoubtedly, clearly
in spite of the fact that	although
in the event that	if, when
in the final analysis	finally
in this day and age	today
in view of the fact that	because
it is clear that	clearly
it is obvious that	obviously
it is my opinion that	(drop completely)
there is no question that	unquestionably, certainly
without a doubt	undoubtedly

5. Check for completeness

The words we use in conversations often have clear references in the environment or context around us. However, in academic and professional writing, some conversational words need to be replaced for full clarity and transparency.

Deictic or pointing words, such as *here, there, this,* and *that,* that are frequently used in spoken language need clear antecedents or full descriptions in writing.

Unclear reference: When traveling by sea, be sure to take that manual.

Clear reference: **When traveling by sea, be sure to take the Morse code manual.**

Intensifiers, such as *so, such,* and *too,* that are used in speech to mean "very" or "exceptionally" usually need an extra phrase or clause to describe **why** something is being intensified.

Unclear reference: Morse code is so out of date.

Clear reference: **Morse code, which was created in the early 1840s, is so out of date that it is rarely used anymore.**

When comparing two or more things in academic writing, be sure to provide both parts of the comparison.

Unclear reference: Semaphore codes are even older.

Clear and full reference: **Semaphore codes, created in the early 1800s, are even older than Morse code, which was first used in the 1840s.**

6. Check for tired, stale, or unnatural language

Descriptive language that is innovative can quickly capture the reader's attention and interest. Note the difference between the following two sentences.

Simple: The boat floated out to sea.

Descriptive: **The rowboat drifted two miles off shore.**

However, writers need to be careful not to get so caught up in description that they borrow the overused expressions of others. As a rule, it is best to stay away from clichés and idioms that have lost their original innovativeness.

Some clichés to avoid	
easier said than done	in a nutshell
face the music	in one ear and out the other
fish out of water	in the nick of time
flat as a pancake	last but not least
food for thought	more than meets the eye
grin and bear it	raining cats and dogs

7. Avoid using pretentious words

It can be tempting for college students to use a thesaurus to add spice to their writing. However, caution should be used when substituting more common, straightforward words with those that sound pretentious, as pretentious words can overshadow the message being conveyed.

Pretentious words	
Instead of...	Try...
aficionado	fan
ascertain	find out
commence	begin
conviviality	friendliness
desist	stop
imbroglio	mess

Pretentious words	
Instead of...	**Try...**
instantiate	support
finalize	finish, complete
impact	affect
jejune	boring, childish
lugubrious	gloomy
methodology	method
nadir	lowest point
optimal	best
peruse	look at, read
potentiate	improve effectiveness
utilize	use

Other Tips to Better Writing

1. Vary basic sentence order

In English, there are seven basic sentence orders for declarative sentences, influenced by different types of verbs and the elements that work with those verbs. Becoming familiar with these basic sentence orders will help you revise your writing if you find yourself frequently writing the same pattern or order.

2. Vary sentence openings

You can vary sentence openings to help your writing not take on a dull or boring sentence rhythm.

Adding in optional introductory words, phrases, or clauses can also lengthen your sentences, a sign of a more sophisticated and complex writing style.

Sample of dull or boring sentence rhythm: The Hollywood sign is a national monument. The Hollywood sign is in Griffith Park in Los Angeles. The sign is 45 feet tall, and it has white letters. It was created as an advertisement in 1923.

Some ways to improve the writing:

Add a transitional/introductory word: The Hollywood sign is a national monument. **However**, it is located in Griffith Park and not Hollywood.

Add an introductory verb phrase: **Located in Griffith Park**, the Hollywood sign is a national monument.

Add an introductory prepositional phrase: **In Griffith Park**, the Hollywood sign is a national monument.

Add an introductory clause:**Although the Hollywood sign was first created as an advertisement in 1923**, it is now a national monument.

3. Fix misplaced modifiers

A modifier (or a word or group of words that describe a noun, adjective, verb, or adverb) can be used to add information to sentences, but they can sometimes cause problems as well if not placed in the correct position in the sentence.

Check for misleading or misplaced modifiers

If a modifier is misplaced, it can cause confusion or even give an unwanted meaning to a sentence. There are three main types of misleading or misplaced modifiers: squinting, limiting, and disruptive.

Squinting modifiers are words or phrases that can refer to more than one word or phrase in the sentence. Revise the sentence so the modifier is placed directly where it refers to only a single word or phrase.

Squinting modifier: The girl in my English class is in the corner with the protest sign.

Is the girl in the corner? Is the protest sign in the corner? Are they both in the corner?

Place the modifier where its meaning cannot be misleading.

OK: **The girl with the protest sign is in the corner; I know her from English class.**

Limiting modifiers, such as *almost, even, just, merely,* and *only,* usually give information about how many or how often. Be careful where you place these modifiers since poor placement can cause ambiguity.

Check for *Dangling modifiers*, which are verbals (to + verb, verb + *–ing,* or verb + *–en/–ed*) placed either at the beginning or end of the sentence and has the verbal modifying the wrong word.

Dangling modifier: **Having been painted**, we put the signs into the   delivery truck.

The dangling modifier (*having been painted*) appears to modify *we,* but it should modify *the signs.* You can fix a dangling modifier in a variety of ways, including moving the word being modified into the correct position or rewording the entire sentence.

OK: **Having been painted**, the signs were put into the delivery truck.

OK: The **painted** signs were put into the truck. OK – We put the **painted** signs into the truck.

Participial verb phrases (with *–ing* or *–ed*) endings are often at the beginning of a dangling modifier.

Dangling modifier: **Left on their own**, the signs were put into the truck by the kids.

OK: The kids, **left on their own**, put the signs into the truck.

4. Check for choppy sentences

Nothing is wrong with a short simple sentence every once in a while; however, many short simple sentences in a row can create a dull and repetitive rhythm that is uncomfortable for the reader. Consider the following sentences.

The Hollywood sign is a national monument. The Hollywood sign is in Griffith Park in Los Angeles. The sign is 45 feet tall. It has white letters. It was created as an advertise- ment in 1923.

What can writers do to rephrase these short and choppy sentences that have the same simple-subject-predicate rhythm? They can join some of the sentences together by using coordinating conjunctions (*for, and, nor, but, or, yet, so*) and creating some compound sentences.

Compound sentences: The Hollywood sign is a national monument, and it is located in Griffith Park in Los Angeles. The sign is 45 feet tall, and it has white letters. It was created as an advertisement

5. Check for excessive coordination

When using compound sentences to bring some variety to writing, one is using a combining strategy that we use quite often in oral language. Be careful, though, that it is not overused in writing since doing so will make it sound too conversational for academic writing.

Too conversational: The Hollywood sign is located in Griffith Park in Los Angeles, and it is 45 feet tall and has white letters, and it was created as an advertisement in 1923.

Use compound sentences sparingly, and mix them with complex sentences or compound-complex sentences to bring more intricacy to your writing.

OK: The Hollywood sign, which is located in Griffith Park in Los Angeles, is 45 feet tall with white letters; it was created as an advertisement in 1923.

6. Avoid commonly confused words

In English, we have many homophones—words that are pronounced the same but have different meanings. Homophones use different spellings, and since this is what distinguishes the meaning, use the dictionary to find the correct word. On the next page is a list of the most commonly misspelled homophones.

Most commonly misspelled homophones	
it's (it is or it has)	its (possessive)
you're (you are)	your (possessive)
they're (they are)	their (possessive), there (place)
who's (who is or who has)	whose (possessive)

Punctuation

Edited by Nichole Stack

Basic punctuation principles exist in written English and other languages to provide general guidelines on how to present different types of phrases and clauses. Learning these basic rules can help you present your writing in a way that is consistent, no matter what you happen to be writing.

Punctuation is a set of conventions generally agreed upon by editors and academics, although some variety in the application of rules may occur across different types of college disciplines or businesses. Punctuation can change the rhythm and speed of your writing, but it can also change meaning. For example, consider how punctuation changes the meaning in the following sentences:

Let's eat, Grandma.

Let's eat Grandma.

In the first sentence, someone is likely inviting Grandma to dinner. In the second sentence, someone is instead inviting us to actually consume poor Grandma. The comma completely changes the meaning, and turns an innocent comment (the first sentence) into a scene from a horror movie (the second sentence).

The basic principles presented in this section can guide you when you have questions about how to use appropriate punctuation at the word or sentence level. This way, you can understand and use the conventions of written English or even change the meanings of sentences as you present them to your reader.

The Comma

Commas are one of the most frequently used punctuation marks. Unfortunately, commas are also the most frequently misused punctuation mark.

Having a reference tool available is always a good idea when you are not sure about how a comma rule applies to your sentence, but the abundance of comma rules can sometimes be frustrating. In this chapter, you will find a few ways to help you use comma rules more effectively.

Remember that comma usage is dictated, first and foremost, by the writer's attempt to communicate meaning. However, comma usage can also be dictated by style guide, or by an author's attempts to craft a message in a particular way for a particular audience.

Set off introductory words, phrases, and clauses

1. Set off introductory words and phrases

Commas are often used to set off introductory words and phrases. If the word or phrase includes a verb, a comma should always be used to separate the word or phrase from the main sentence.

Shocked, Alex put out his cigarette when he saw the new No Smoking sign.

Frustrated by the new sign, Alex put out his cigarette.

If the introductory word is a single preposition or adverb, you may omit the comma.

Yesterday the guests grumbled about the new sign.

If the introductory prepositional phrase is short (usually viewed as being five words or fewer), you may also omit the comma.

Below the stage the guests grumbled about the new sign.

Note that your decision to include or omit the comma is a "heuristic," a rule of thumb (not to be confused with a rigid "algorithm"). The author should be striving to ensure that he/she has used the comma to create the proper meaning.

2. Set off introductory clauses

Always use a comma after an introductory clause. The use of a verb in any kind of introductory word, phrase, or clause is the clue to always use a comma.

Since he had recently quit smoking, Alex was happy to see the new No Smoking sign.

Although Chris was unhappy about the new sign, Alex was quite content.

Combine independent clauses in compound sentences

A comma is used between two independent clauses that are joined by a coordinating conjunction, such as any of the FANBOYS—*for, and, nor, but, or, yet, so.*

Independent clause/simple sentence – Chris was unhappy about the new sign.

Independent clause/simple sentence – Alex was quite content about the new sign.

Compound sentence – Chris was unhappy about the new sign, **but** Alex was quite content.

Be sure that the clauses on each side of the comma + conjunction are independent. A comma is never used between conjoined noun phrases or conjoined verb phrases.

Review of Basic Punctuation and Mechanics

Misused comma – Chris, and Alex had a terrible argument outside the building.

OK – Chris and Alex had a terrible argument outside the building.

Misused comma – Chris was unhappy about the sign, and left campus early.

OK – Chris was unhappy about the sign and left campus early.

You can sometimes omit the comma when the two clauses are short. This can create a quicker rhythm or speed in the sentence. Including the comma, however, can place additional emphasis on each of the ideas.

Quicker Sentence – Chris was unhappy and he left.

Comma Creates Emphasis – Chris was unhappy, and he left.

Separate items in a series: the "Oxford Comma"

Commas are used to separate words, phrases, or clauses in a series. This is often referred to as the "Oxford Comma." A "series" is a list of at least three items that are parallel with each other (e.g., three nouns or three phrases).

Chris, Alex, and Max spent three hours arguing about the new signs around campus.

Outside the building, I saw **two teachers, Chris, and Alex**.

Chris **talked, cajoled, and yelled** as he tried to convince the administrators.

As I left the building, Max was **taking down the sign, yelling at some strangers, and jumping up and down**.

The Oxford comma allows the reader to see each item individually. Without it, the reader might accidentally combine certain elements. For instance, take a look at the second sentence. If I omitted the Oxford comma, the sentence would look like this: "Outside the building, I saw two teachers, Chris and Alex." In the original sentence, the author is describing four total people: two teachers, Chris, and Alex. In the rewritten sentence, the author is describing only two people: Chris and Alex, both of whom are teachers. The meaning has completely changed.

If the items in a series that you are connecting already have commas, use semi-colons to separate them. See the **semi-colon** section for further discussion of how/ when to use a semi-colon.

When the campus police arrived, they wanted to ticket Chris, who began the argument; Alex, who escalated the argument; and Max, who threw the first punch.

Set off non-essential elements

Commas can be used to enclose non-essential information that is included in a sentence. To be non-essential, the information needs to be unnecessary for a reader to understand the central meaning of the sentence.

1. Relative clauses

Relative clauses can be essential or non-essential when it comes to understanding the main meaning of the full sentence. Relative clauses that are not necessary are non-restrictive and need to be set off by commas.

Chris and Alex, **who were in my English class**, were arguing violently.

In the above sentence, the information about which class Chris and Alex were in is non-essential to the meaning of the independent clause.

If a relative clause is essential to the full meaning of the sentence, it is restrictive and should not have any commas around it.

The audience **that was closest to Chris and Alex** was getting violent as well.

In the sentence above, the relative clause ("that was closest to Chris and Alex") is essential information. It was just the audience closest to Chris and Alex who were getting violent, not those in the audience farther away.

Using *that* for non-essential relative clauses and a comma plus a relative pronoun, such as *which* or *who*, for essential relative clauses is a way that some editors and writers help distinguish between non-essential and essential sentence elements. If you are required to follow MLA (Modern Language Association) or APA (American

Psychological Association) guidelines, follow this convention. However, even MLA acknowledges that some writers do not follow this convention, so it's a good idea to check with your instructor about this grammar rule.

Remember, though, that punctuation works together with meaning. Two sentences that look almost the same can use different punctuation due to the meaning the writer has in mind.

> Non-restrictive relative clause – Tennessee, **which is a beautiful state**, has all the signs of a bad economy.

> Restrictive relative clause – I like the Tennessee **that is a beautiful state** and not the one **that has signs of a bad economy**.

In the first sentence above, the main idea of the sentence can be understood without the relative clause *which is a beautiful state*. This makes the relative clause non-essential, requiring commas. In the second sentence, the main idea of the sentence can only be understood with the two relative clauses *that is a beautiful state* and *that has signs of a bad economy* included. This makes the two relative clauses essential, thus requiring no commas.

2. Participial phrases

Participial phrases are verb phrases that describe nouns. They take commas wherever they occur—at the beginning of the sentence, in the middle of the sentence, or at the end of the sentence.

> Sentence with participial phrase – The Hollywood sign, **first built in 1923**, was restored in 1978 with money from Gene Autry, Alice Cooper, and others.

> Sentence with participial phrase – The Hollywood sign, **located in Griffith Park and not Hollywood**, was restored in 1978 with money from Gene Autry, Alice Cooper, and others.

3. Appositives

Appositives are nouns, noun phrases, and noun clauses that rename nouns. The same restrictive/non-restrictive comma rule that applies to relative clauses applies to appositives (see **15d** for more information on restrictive and non-restrictive elements).

> Sentence with non-restrictive appositive – The Hollywood sign, **a national monument**, was restored in 1978 with money from Gene Autry, Alice Cooper, and others.

> Sentence with restrictive appositive – The musician **Alice Cooper** helped fund the restoration of the Hollywood sign.

Review of Basic Punctuation and Mechanics

Separate coordinate adjectives

A comma is used to separate coordinate adjectives. Adjectives are considered coordinate when they directly and equally modify a noun phrase. One test to see whether you are using coordinate adjectives is to reverse their order—if the original modification relationship exists, you have coordinate adjectives. Another test to see whether you are using coordinate adjectives is to place an *and* between the two adjectives—once again, if the original meaning exists, you have coordinate adjectives.

> Sam and Alex saw the **dull, unappealing** billboard for the movie and changed their minds about seeing it.
>
> Sam and Alex saw the **unappealing, dull** billboard for the movie and changed their minds about seeing it.

Set off interrupters

1. *Transitions*

When an adverbial conjunction (also called a conjunctive adverb) appears in the middle of a sentence, it is separated off from the main sentence with commas.

> The Hollywood sign, **moreover**, does not include any of the original letters.
>
> Alice Cooper, **however**, donated money for the renovation in honor of Groucho Marx.
>
> Addition – moreover, furthermore, likewise, finally, additionally, also, incidentally
>
> Contrast – however, nevertheless, in contrast, on the contrary, nonetheless, otherwise, on the other hand, in comparison, conversely, instead
>
> Comparison – similarly, likewise
>
> Exemplification – for example, for instance
>
> Intensification – indeed, in fact, moreover, still, certainly
>
> Result – therefore, thus, consequently, as a result, finally, then, accordingly, hence, subsequently, undoubtedly
>
> Time – meanwhile, then, next, finally, still, now

It is important to note, however, that adverbial conjunctions should not be used to connect two independent clauses. They do not function in the same way as conjunctions (words such as *or*, *but*, or *and*), which can connect two independent clauses. For instance, check out the following sentences:

> **Correct**: I liked the steak, **but** I didn't like the salad.
>
> **Incorrect**: I liked the steak, **however**, I didn't like the salad.

Adverbial conjunctions should only be used in the middle of the sentence if they can also be used at the start of the sentence:

> **Correct: However**, I didn't like the salad.
>
> **Correct**: I didn't, **however**, like the salad.

2. *Interjections*

A comma is used to mark or enclose a weak exclamation or interjection, separating it from the rest of the sentence. An interjection can come at the beginning, in the middle, or at the end of a sentence.

For **goodness sake**, the instruction book about traffic signs is over 20 pages long.

The instruction book about traffic signs is over 20 pages long, **for goodness sake**.

I do not understand, **for goodness sake**, why that book about traffic signs is so long.

3. Direct address

A comma is used to mark or enclose a noun phrase that is used as a direct address. When you use a noun phrase that names the person or persons being spoken to, you are using the form of a direct address.

"**Sam**, did you see the billboard for *Terminator: Salvation*?"

"Did you see the billboard for *Terminator: Salvation*, **Sam**?"

"I thought the billboard for *Jumper* was good, **Sam**, but did you see the one for *Terminator: Salvation*?"119

4. Tag questions

Commas are also used to mark tags, which are added to the end of a sentence to question whether the statement that precedes the tag is accurate or not.

The poster for *Sherlock Holmes* made the main character look somewhat dastardly, **didn't it**?

It has been a long time since we have had a modern Sherlock Holmes, **hasn't it**?

Set off quotations or dialogue

Commas are used to set off a speaker's words from the rest of the sentence.

Chris complained "**That book is over 20 pages long**."

"**That book is over 20 pages long**," Chris complained.

"**That book**," Chris complained, "**is over 20 pages long**." Commas are not used with indirect quotations or speech.

Chris complained that the book was too long.

Commas are not used after an exclamation point or question mark.

"That book is too long!" complained Chris.

"How long is that book on traffic signs?" asked Chris with a frown on his face.

Set off geographic locations

Commas are used to set off items in an address or in the name of a place.

Please send any comments about the new sign to Department of Signage, Box 50, Fairbanks, Alaska 99701.

Murfreesboro, Tennessee, is near Nashville.

Be sure to check out the new sign at The Stone's River Mall, Murfreesboro, Tennessee.

A comma is never used between the name of a state and a Zip Code.

> You should send your card and return postage to the Department of Signage, Box 50, Fairbanks, AK 99701.

Set off dates

Commas are used to set off items in a date. Use commas between the day and month, the date and year, and the year and the rest of the sentence.

> The smoking signs were changed on Monday, January 1, 2010, when the new law took effect.

A comma is never used between the date and month or the month and year when the date is written in inverted order.

> The smoking signs were changed on Monday, 1 January 2010, when the new law took effect.

A comma is never used when only the month and year are given.

> The smoking signs were changed in January 2010.

Set off titles

A comma is used to set off a person's title or degree.

> Dr. Watson had a sign outside his front door that said John H. Watson, M.D.
>
> Juliet Freestone, PhD, noted expert on Sherlock Holmes, will speak at the library today.

Commas are not always used for Jr., Sr., II, or III, which are considered part of someone's name. This rule is in flux; check with your instructor about his or her preference, and consult a style guide for further variations.

> Robert Downey, Jr. played Sherlock Holmes in the film by the same name.
>
> Robert Downey Jr. played Sherlock Holmes in the film by the same name.

Set off numbers

When numbers are longer than four digits, use commas to separate them, placing a comma every three numbers starting from the right.

> 1,000
>
> 1,000,000
>
> 1,000,000,000

Do not use commas in the above way when writing years, telephone numbers, street addresses, or zip codes.

Prevent confusion

Most grammar handbooks will tell you to use commas to prevent confusion. These might be the kinds of examples shared with you.

What Chris did, did affect all of us.

It was the sign she had waited for, for years.

However, if you find yourself needing to use a comma to avoid confusion, you probably need to revise the entire sentence.

What Chris did that day affected all of us.

She had waited for years for the sign.

The Semi-Colon

A semi-colon connects phrases or clauses that are closely linked in meaning. Using a semi-colon is limited to three situations.

Connect independent clauses

Semi-colons can connect two independent clauses (or simple sentences) to form a compound sentence.

Simple sentence/independent clause – The Chinese zodiac uses twelve animals to represent human qualities.

Simple sentence/independent clause – The Chinese zodiac runs on a twelve-year cycle.

Compound sentence – The Chinese zodiac uses twelve animals to represent human qualities; it also runs on a twelve- year cycle.

Use with adverbial conjunctions or transitional phrases to connect clauses

Two simple sentences can be connected with an adverbial conjunction (also known as a conjunctive adverb) when a semi-colon is used to the left of the adverbial conjunction and a comma to the right of it. See **15f** for a list of adverbial conjunctions.

The Chinese zodiac uses twelve animals to represent human qualities; **furthermore**, it runs on a twelve-year cycle.

The Chinese zodiac uses twelve animals to represent human qualities; **in fact**, it runs on a twelve-year cycle.

Separate groups that contain commas

If the items in a series that you are connecting already have commas, use semi-colons to separate them.

The Chinese zodiac uses twelve animals, such as the boar and the snake, to represent human qualities; runs on a twelve- year cycle; and is widely used throughout Asia, not just in China.

The Colon

A colon has a variety of uses, but its overall function is to connect elements while still keeping them slightly separated from each other.

Nearly all formatting guidelines will suggest using one space after a colon.

According to the MLA, the first letter of the word that follows a colon should be lower-case, unless that word is one that is normally capitalized or is part of a rule, principle, or quotation. However, according to the APA, the first letter of the sentence following a colon should be upper-case if the sentence is an independent clause. Since the rule for using capitalization with a colon can change across documentation styles, it's a good idea to ask your instructor for clarification about which style is prefered.

Connect independent clauses

A colon is used to connect two independent clauses (or simple sentences) when the first clause introduces a definition, expanded description, or specific information that clarifies what was introduced in the first clause.

The Chinese zodiac uses twelve animals and runs on a twelve-year cycle: the animals represent different qualities of human nature, such as calmness or righteousness.

Add emphasis

Colons can be used to emphasize words, phrases, or clauses.

When I first studied the Chinese zodiac, I could not believe my sign: **the pig**.

Introduce a series or list

A colon is used to introduce a list or a series of words or phrases. As you can see in the sentence below, on the left side of the colon is an independent clause.

The Chinese zodiac also describes its animal signs with four elements: **fire, metal, water, and wood**.

Colons should not follow phrases like *such as, for example, includes,* or *including.* In fact, no punctuation should be used after these phrases when giving a list.

Correct: The Chinese zodiac has signs **such as roosters, snakes, and boars.**

Incorrect: The Chinese zodiac has signs **such as: roosters, snakes, and boars.**

Introduce a quotation or saying

A colon should be used to introduce a quotation or saying when it is a complete sentence.

> I have a Chinese proverb by which I live: **"When you only have two pennies left in the world, buy a loaf of bread with one and a lily with the other."**

Use for salutations in formal letters

In a formal business letter, the colon is commonly used in the salutation. A comma can be used for personal letters.

Dear Judge Smith:

Connect numbers

Colons are used for connecting numbers in a variety of ways.

1. Connect ratios

The ratio of sunny days to snow days is 45:1.

2. Connect chapters and verses of holy texts

Ezra 6:18

Job 29:4

Qur'an 3:3

Vedanta-sutra 4:1:12

3. Connect hours, minutes, and seconds

11:05:01

3:13 a.m.

7:03 p.m.

Connect titles and subtitles

The Chinese Zodiac: Twelve Personalities Represented by Animals

The Period, Exclamation Point, and Question Mark

Choosing end punctuation is easy if you know the type and function of the sentence you are writing. Writers use declarative sentences to give information, imperative sentences to give instructions or commands, interrogative sentences to obtain information, and exclamatory sentences to express emotion.

Declarative sentence or statement – The Chinese zodiac has four elements.

Imperative sentence or command – Tell me which zodiac sign I am.

Interrogative sentence or question – How many Chinese zodiac signs are there?

Exclamatory sentence or exclamation –You're a Boar! Really!

Use a period to end a sentence or separate initials or abbreviations

1. End a sentence

When crafting a declarative sentence that gives information, makes a statement, or gives a mild command, use a period to end the sentence.

Gives information – In the Chinese zodiac, different animals rule each year.

Makes a statement – The Chinese zodiac is fascinating, especially when it is compared to our Western zodiac.

Gives a mild command – Learn the animals and elements of the Chinese zodiac for the quiz tomorrow.

2. Separate initials or abbreviations

Periods are placed after an initial or an abbreviation.

Ms. Smith, Mr. Smith, Mrs. Smith, Dr. Allison D. Smith, Adam

A. Smith, Jr., Sen. Thomas P. Smith, Prof. Adam Smith, Rev. Smith

Using periods for the above list is always correct.

The following abbreviations can appear with or without periods, depending upon the author's (or reader's) preference.

BA, BS, MA, PhD

GP, LPN, MBA, MD, RN

BC, BCE, AD, CE, AM, PM

States can often be abbreviated in a variety of ways, including some forms that take periods. For instance, *PA* or *Penn.* can be used for the state of Pennsylvania. However, in formal writing, it is not commonly accepted that states be abbreviated in any way except in complete addresses.

Emphasize with an exclamation point

An exclamation mark is used at the end of an exclamatory sentence to express a strong feeling or to give emphasis.

This is the last time I will comment. Stop asking me!

Imagine! The foundation of astrology goes back thousands of years.

End a direct question, show uncertainty, or embed a short question with a question mark

1. *End a direct question*

A question mark is used at the end of a direct question or interrogative.

Are there any similarities between the Chinese zodiac and Western astrology?

2. *Show uncertainty*

A question mark can also be used to show uncertainty about a fact or piece of information. When used this way, the question mark should be placed within parentheses.

Western astrology began in the 2nd century AD (?).

3. *Embed a short question within the middle of a sentence*

A short question can be embedded within a longer sentence in three ways: within parentheses, enclosed by dashes, or just within the sentence itself.

Western astrology began in the 2nd century AD (is this similar to Chinese astrology?) and has twelve signs.

Western astrology began in the 2nd century AD—is this similar to Chinese astrology?—and has twelve signs.

When she asked the question, why are Western and Chinese zodiacs so similar? at the lecture, the speaker gave her a point-by-point answer.

The Apostrophe

The apostrophe is used in a variety of situations and is one of the most complicated punctuation marks to use.

Unless you know for sure that your usage is correct, it's a good idea to consult your instructor or your style guide (MLA or APA) to double-check its use during your editing sessions.

Mark omissions when parts of words are removed

An apostrophe is used to show that one or more letters have been omitted. For instance, use an apostrophe to show in *I'm* that the *a* has been deleted.

1. Mark contractions when parts of words are removed

I'm, you're, he's, she's, it's, they're, we're

I hadn't, you haven't

I can't, I couldn't, you won't, you wouldn't, they'll, they shouldn't

2. Mark numbers when parts of numbers are removed

in the year '95

3. Mark words used to represent oral language

When using unusual or informal spellings to represent oral language, you can use apostrophes to mark contractions.

a-walkin', trekin', y'all

Form plurals

The MLA recommends that an apostrophe along with an –*s* be used to create the plural of abbreviations that include lowercase letters, uppercase letters, or both.

A's, B's, C's, D's, E's, PhD's, Mind your P's and Q's!

However, many instructors prefer that no apostrophe be used at all.

As, Bs, Cs, Ds, Es, PhDs, Mind your Ps and Qs

Some instructors may prefer that you italicize the letter and use regular font style for the –*s* ending.

*A*s, *B*s, *C*s, *D*s, *E*s

It is best to check with your instructor on how he or she wants you to format letters.

Apostrophes, in general, should not be used to form the plurals of numbers, abbreviations or acronyms that include all uppercase letters, and phrases that refer to words.

1980s, the 60s

TAs, CEOs, IOUs

She uses many ands but not enough other conjunctions in her writing.

Form possessives

An apostrophe is used in various ways to form possessives. Knowing the difference between singular nouns, indefinite pronouns, and plural nouns will help you use the apostrophe correctly.

1. Form singular possessives

- **Singular nouns**

  An apostrophe and –s can be added to most singular nouns and acronyms to form the possessive.

  Sam's book, the student's pen, the new sign's message

  the CEO's email, MLA's style guide

- **Personal pronouns**

  Personal pronouns do not take an apostrophe since they already show possession.

  my, your, yours, his, her, hers, its, our, ours, their, theirs

- **Indefinite pronouns**

  An apostrophe and an –s is used at the end of an indefinite pronoun to show possession.

  anyone's, anybody's, everyone's, everybody's, someone's, somebody's

2. Mark plural possessives

Plural nouns that do not end in –s take an apostrophe plus an –s to form the possessive. Plural nouns that end in –s only take the apostrophe.

the children's song, the geese's honk, the data's collection

the cats' meows, the judges' decision, the zodiacs' signs, the Smiths' house , the Joneses' cat

3. Form possessive compound nouns

When a sentence includes conjoined nouns, the type of ownership or possession determines how to use the apostrophe. If each noun has separate ownership, each noun is marked by the possessive. If the nouns have ownership together, only the last noun is made possessive by using the apostrophe.

Separate ownership – Sam's and Alex's zodiac signs are not compatible.

Joint ownership – Jack and Jill's pail fell down the hill.

Form compounds

An apostrophe and –s is placed at the end of a compound word when signaling possession.

my mother-in-law's sign, mother-of-pearl's color

An apostrophe and *–s* can be placed at the end of a plural compound word, or the possession can be signaled with an *of* phrase.

my brothers-in-law's zodiac signs

the zodiac signs of my brothers-in-law

Quotation Marks

Quotation marks are used in a variety of situations as described below.

Generally, when a quotation mark falls at the end of a clause or sentence, place periods and commas inside the quotation mark.

My instructor assigned us a new story entitled "Signs and Symbols."

When I read "Signs and Symbols," I was reminded of a story from my childhood.

When you create an in-text citation (in MLA format), the period follows the citation in parentheses.

Margaret Jones, in her essay on sign language, says that "anyone who really wants to learn sign language can do so relatively easily" (101).

Signal titles of short works

Quotation marks are used to enclose the titles of short works, including poems, short stories, lectures, book chapters, song titles, magazine articles, newspaper articles, encyclopedia entries, and television/radio episodes.

"Pedestrians Not Permitted on this Highway" – a poem by Jackson H. Day

"Signs and Symbols" – a short story by Vladimir Nabokov

"The Signs of Life" – a lecture by Augustus D. Waller, MD

"Signs Inconjunct" – a book chapter by Ptolemy

"Signs" – a song by Five Man Electrical Band

"Swine Flu Myth: The Symptoms Are Like Regular Flu" – a magazine article

"CDC: Swine Flu Outbreak Signs Encouraging" – a newspaper article

"Sign Language (Communications)" – an encyclopedia entry

"Born Under a Bad Sign" – episode from television's *Supernatural*

Set off a direct quotation

Quotation marks are also used to set off direct quotations.

"The thunderstorm last night was the first sign of spring," said the ABC weatherman.

Albert Einstein said, "The true sign of intelligence is not knowledge but imagination."

Set off dialogue in prose

Quotation marks are used to set off dialogue. Be sure to use a separate paragraph for each speaker, and use quotation marks around everything each person says.

from *Signs* (2002 film):

"What kind of a machine bends a stalk of corn without breaking it?" asked Officer Caroline.

Graham responded, "It can't be by hand; it's too perfect."

Share a few lines of poetry

Quotation marks are used when quoting four or fewer lines of poetry. Be sure to enclose all material from the poem in quotation marks, and use a slash—with a space on each side of the slash—to show where the original line was divided. When quoting material from a source, be sure to give the documentation information.

I cannot help but compare my visit to the lines of one of my favorite poems by Jackson H. Day called "Wesley Theological Seminary: No Thoroughfare": "**O you who see this sign, pray it may go/And all it represents; and later, lo/This path can be the broadest thoroughfare**" (II.4-6).

Share personal thoughts

During the visit, I could not help but compare my reception to the metaphor of a favorite poem: "**I wish these people would think about how they could create the broadest of thoroughfares.**"

Signal something being discussed, defined, or used in an unusual or ironic manner

I never thought there were so many sentences with the word "**sign**" in them.

Joe has been "**signing off**" to his girlfriend lately, meaning that he has been showing off.

At the bar, when Joe said his "**sign**" meant he was open for business, I had to laugh.

The Hyphen

· ·
The hyphen is used in a variety of situations as described below.
· ·

Join words to make compound adjectives

A hyphen is used to join two adjectives into a compound adjective before a noun. Do not use a hyphen between the two adjectives when they follow a verb and are not in front of a noun to describe it.

freeze-dried coffee, red-light district, well-lighted sign, carry-on luggage

She can't tolerate coffee that is **freeze dried**.

Connect prefixes and suffixes to root words

Join certain prefixes (*all-, ex-, half-,* and *self-*) to a root word

all-inclusive, ex-husband, half-back, self-starter

Link a single letter to a noun or participle

A hyphen can also be used to join single letters to a noun or participle.

X-ray, y-axis, U-turn, G-rated

Join words to make compound numbers

A hyphen is used to join compound numbers from *twenty-one* to *ninety-nine*.

twenty-one, thirty-two, forty-three, forty-four

Join numbers

Hyphens are used to join the numerator and denominator in a fraction. They are also used to give a person's life span or a score.

one-fourth, two-thirds, four-fifths

Edward Minor Gallaudet (1837-1917) was the founder and first president of a university for the deaf.

In last night's bowling championship, Smith beat Jones 222-219.

Prevent confusion

A hyphen should be used to avoid awkward spelling or confusion when using a prefix or suffix.

pre-eminent, re-educate, anti-infective

The football player will re-sign. vs. The football player will resign.

The Dash

The dash is used in a variety of ways. Much like a set of parentheses, it can interrupt a sentence to offer additional explanation. And much like a colon, it can be used to signal a definition or a list.

The three main uses for the dash are highlighted previously.

The dash should not be confused with the hyphen, though. To create a dash, you will need to use *two strokes* of the hyphen key, without spacing before or after.

Highlight introductory material

A dash can be used to highlight introductory material. Usually, the clause that follows the dash will give further explanation about the introductory material.

A pig or a boar—those are the two names for my Chinese zodiac sign.

Set off parenthetical, explanatory, or contrasted material

I cannot accept either name—a pig or boar—for my Chinese zodiac sign.

Chinese zodiac signs—based on animals and natural elements—describe general qualities of a person's nature.

I'd much rather be a dragon—not a pig—for my Chinese zodiac sign.

Add emphasis

Dashes can be used instead of commas when you want to add emphasis to something.

I still can't believe what my Chinese zodiac sign is—a pig or boar!

Parentheses

A parenthesis (the singular form of "parentheses") is a type of bracket, and interrupts a sentence. Often, it can function in similar ways to the dash (described in the previous section), but there are also a number of other circumstances for which you might need to use a set of parentheses.

Enclose explanatory, minor, or secondary information

Parentheses are used to add material that might interrupt the flow of the sentence. The added information is considered secondary or minor to the main idea of the sentence.

In the Chinese zodiac, a person with the boar (a pig) sign is honest, sociable, and hardworking.

Enclose in-text citations

Parentheses are also used to enclose in-text citations when you need to document your source(s).

MLA in-text citation – Williams theorizes that the overlap in different systems of astrology is due to "the inherent relationship between travel and storytelling" (234).

APA in-text citation – Williams theorizes that the overlap in different systems of astrology is due to "the inherent relationship between travel and storytelling" (p. 234).

Enclose numbers or letters in outlines

Parentheses can be used at different levels of outlines to enclose numbers or letters.

(1)
(2)

Brackets

Use square brackets to signal corrections or errors

1. Signal editorial correction

Square brackets are usually used to signal that an editorial correction or clarification has been made within a quotation.

"The inherent relationship between [the Chinese and Western] systems of astrology is due to exploration and storytelling" (Williams 234).

2. Signal editorial error

Square brackets that are placed around the word *sic* ("as such" in Latin) signal that an editorial error was made by the original writer or speaker.

"The inherent relationship between [*sic*] the three systems of astrology is due to exploration and storytelling" (Williams 234).

Use angle brackets to signal Web addresses

Angle brackets (< >) are used to signal Web addresses and separate them unmistakably from the rest of the sentence.

Angle brackets also allow for the end punctuation to fall outside the brackets, thus not creating any confusion about whether the end punctuation is part of the Web address.

To learn more about Chinese astrology, visit <http://chinesezo- diac.com>.

The Slash

The slash (/) is often called the forward slash to distinguish it from the backslash (\) used in Web addresses. It is also sometimes called the diagonal or the oblique.

Quote lines of poetry

When quoting more than one line of poetry, the slash (or diagonal) is used to show where each line of poetry ends. Be sure to place a space on each side of the slash.

I cannot help but compare my visit to the lines of a favorite poem by Jackson H. Day called "Wesley Theological Seminary: No Thoroughfare": "**O you who see this sign, pray it may go / And all it represents; and later, lo / This path can be the broadest thoroughfare**" (II.4-6).

Show a choice

A slash can also be used between two words to show that either choice is available or acceptable.

the in/out door, the up/down button

Ellipses

Ellipses (or ellipsis points) consist of three periods that are spaced equally apart. They are used in quotations to indicate that words have been omitted. Different style guides might suggest different spacing between the periods.

Signal omissions

Original – "My attitude towards punctuation is that it ought to be as conventional as possible. The game of golf would lose a good deal if croquet mallets and billiard cues were allowed on the putting green. You ought to be able to show that you can do it a good deal better than anyone else with the regular tools before you have a license to bring in your own improvements."

–Ernest Hemingway

Quotation – "My attitude towards punctuation is that it ought to be as conventional as possible… You ought to be able to show that you can do it a good deal better than anyone else…before you have a license to bring in your own improvements."

When quoting poetry, use a line of ellipsis points to signal that you have dropped a line or more of the poem.

Signal a pause or hesitation

Ellipses can also be used to signal a pause or hesitation.

I wish…that punctuation was as conventional as possible, just as Hemingway describes it.

Signal a trail-off

Ellipses can also be used to signal that the speaker is "trailing off," losing focus, or fading.

"I'm not sure where I put the…" he said.

Capitalization

Capitalization is necessary in a variety of situations as described below.

Indicate the first word

1. Indicate the first word in a sentence

Capitalization is used for the first word in every sentence.

Traffic signs are sometimes difficult to understand.

2. Indicate the first word in a quotation

Capitalization is also used to indicate the first word in a quotation.

My brother told the police officer, "**But** the sign was covered by a tree branch."

3. Indicate the first word inside parentheses

Capitalization is used when a full sentence is placed within parentheses. If the parenthetical statement is inserted into another sentence, do not capitalize.

My brother told the officer that the sign was covered by a tree branch. (**However, it wasn't.**)

My brother told the officer (**from our father's precinct**) that the sign was covered by a tree branch.

My brother told the officer (**the officer was from our father's precinct**) that the sign was covered by a tree branch.

4. Indicate the first word in a sentence following a colon

Capitalization after a colon is optional; however, capitalize the first word after a colon if you want to emphasize the sentence.

My brother has had several tickets: **he** has been caught driving with a broken headlight, driving too fast in a school zone, and not stopping for a pedestrian in the crosswalk.

The police officer voided the ticket: **He** was from our father's precinct.

Indicate proper nouns and proper adjectives

Capitalization is used to indicate proper nouns and proper adjectives.

1. Indicate proper nouns

Proper nouns name specific people, places, things, or ideas. For more information on proper nouns, see **2b**.

People –Abigail Breslin, Joaquin Phoenix, Aunt Joan, Uncle Ralph, Senator Jones, Reverend Smith, Dr. Black, Chief Johnson, Professor White

Places – Europe, Australia, Alaska, Washington, D.C., the South, the Northeast, the Mississippi River, the Grand Canyon, New York City, United States

Organizations, governmental institutions, and academic institutions –Federal Bureau of Investigation, Department of Labor, the United Nations, Long Beach City College, Harvard University

Abbreviations of titles and organizations – AAA, FBI, MD, MLA, PhD, UN, UCLA

Monuments and buildings – the Washington Monument, the Willis Tower, the Taj Mahal, the Eiffel Tower

Languages – Chinese, English, Arabic, Swahili, Spanish, French, Japanese, Russian, Mandarin, American Sign Language

Races – American Indian, Alaskan Native, Pacific Islander, African American, Black, White, Asian

Nationalities – Spanish, Ethiopian, Arabic, Chinese, South African, Greek, American

Religions and religious terms – Buddhism, Islam, Christianity, Judaism, Shinto, Protestant, Catholic, Baptist, Buddha, Mohammed, God, Jesus, Moses, Talmud, Bible, Koran, Allah, Jehovah, Genesis

Course titles – English 101, Biology 1001, French 300, English Composition 101, Modern War Ethics, An Introduction to Computer History

Days and months – January, March, May, Sunday, Tuesday, Thursday

2. Indicate proper adjectives

Capitalization is also used for proper adjectives, which are usually derived from proper nouns and can be found inside a proper noun phrase.

Chinese food, English language, Spanish eyes

Indicate titles and subtitles

Capitalization is used for titles of books, stories, plays, poems, songs, articles, films, newspapers, magazines, works of art, musical compositions, and photographs. Always capitalize the first word in the title, no matter the type of word. Also, if using MLA (Modern Language Association) style, capitalize all other words in the title or subtitle except for articles (*a, an, the*), conjunctions (*for, and, nor, but, or, yet, so*), and short prepositions (*in, on, for, to*). If using another style, such as from the APA (American Psychological Association), be sure to check specific guidelines.

Books – *The World According to Garp*

Books with subtitles – *Chinese Astrology: Exploring the Eastern Zodiac*

Short stories – "Everyday Use" Plays – *Hamlet*

Poems – "Casey at Bat"

Songs – "Rudolph, the Red-Nosed Reindeer"

Articles – "Fifty Ways to Avoid the Flu"

Films – *Moulin Rouge*

Newspapers – *The New York Times*

Magazines and journals – *Vogue, English Journal*

Works of art – *Starry Night*

Musical compositions – *Romeo et Juliette*

Photographs – *The Kiss*

Vessels – *Spruce Goose, Queen Mary*

Indicate acronyms

Acronyms are made up of the first letter of each word in a phrase. For instance, *FBI* is the acronym for "Federal Bureau of Investigation." Acronyms are usually capitalized except for those that have become regular words such as *scuba*, *laser*, and *radar*.

Acronyms – CBS, CEO, CIA, FAQ, SAT, USA, WGN

Italics

· ·
Italics are used to emphasize special words, phrases, or clauses.
· ·

If you are writing by hand or are unable to use italics, you can underline the items that should be in italics.

Highlight titles

1. Highlight titles of longer works

To highlight the title of a larger or longer work, use italics. Thus, you should italicize the titles of poetry or short story collections, anthologies, books, albums/CDs, magazines, newspapers, encyclopedias, television series, and radio series.

Signs of Life: A Book of Visual Poetry by John Ecko

Vital Signs: International Short Stories on Aging by Dorothy Sennett and Anne Czarniecki

The Signs of Language Revisited: An Anthology in Honor of Ursula Bellugi and Edward Klima – edited by Karen Emmorey and Harlan L. Lane

Lonely Planet Signspotting – a book by Doug Lansky

The Sign – a CD by Ace of Base

Vital Signs – a magazine

Encyclopedia Britannica – an encyclopedia

Sign of the Times – a television series

The Bob and Tom Radio Show – a radio series

2. Highlight legal cases

Italics are used to highlight the titles of legal cases.

Roe v. Wade, Brown v. Board of Education of Topeka, State v. Scopes

3. Identify naval and air ships

Italics are used to identify naval crafts, aircraft, and spacecraft.

Nimitz, Titanic, Queen Mary

Spruce Goose, Spirit of St. Louis, Lockheed Vega, Air Force One

Challenger, Atlantis, Enterprise, Sputnik, Explorer

Highlight special letters, words, phrases, or clauses

Italics are used to highlight special letters, words, phrases, and clauses.

1. Highlight non-English words

Italics are used when you write a non-English word or phrase. If the word or phrase is used multiple times, use italics only the first time it is used.

French phrase for "joy of living" – Every time I see Karen, I drink in her *joie de vivre*.

Japanese word for "special singing and dancing" – My favorite part of Japanese night was the *kabuki* theater.

Arabic phrase for "have a safe journey" – As he left me on the trail, the guide wished me, "*Bissalama*."

The English language has borrowed heavily from other languages for centuries, and some of these words are now considered part of English. For these types of everyday words, you do not use italics.

soy (Japanese), glasnost (Russian), banana (Wolof), Kwanzaa (Swahili), cider (Hebrew)

2. Highlight referenced or discussed letters, words, phrases, and clauses

You also use italics to highlight words that you are discussing, defining, or using in a special way.

Words with the letters *SK* at the beginning are usually of Scandinavian origin.

I had no idea that the word *banana* came from the African language Wolof.

Leviathan had the original meaning of "sea monster" but now refers to anything of an unusual size.

Index